FORGOTTEN HIGHWAYS

Forgotten Highways

WILDERNESS JOURNEYS DOWN THE
HISTORIC TRAILS OF THE CANADIAN ROCKIES

by Nicky Brink and Stephen R. Bown

BRINDLE
& GLASS

Library and Archives Canada Cataloguing in Publication
Brink, Nicky L.
Forgotten highways : wilderness journeys down the historic
trails of the Canadian Rockies / Nicky L. Brink and Stephen R. Bown.

Includes index. ISBN 978-1-897142-24-0

1. Brink, Nicky L.—Travel—Rocky Mountains, Canadian (B.C. and Alta.).
2. Bown, Stephen R.--Travel--Rocky Mountains, Canadian (B.C. and Alta.).
3. Historic roads and trails--Rocky Mountains, Canadian (B.C. and Alta.).
4. Trails--Rocky Mountains, Canadian (B.C. and Alta.). 5. Explorers—Rocky Mountains, Canadian (B.C. and Alta.)--Biography. 6. Rocky Mountains, Canadian (B.C. and Alta.)--Discovery and exploration. 7. Rocky Mountains, Canadian (B.C. and Alta.)--Description and travel. I. Bown, Stephen R. II. Title.

FC219.B747 2007   917.1104   C2007-901860-2

Cover images, top: H. J. Warre
Cover image, bottom, all modern interior images and author photo copyright the authors. Historical images are in the public domain.
Maps: David Bown, High Country Web Design, www.high-country.ca
To see the *Forgotten Highways* photos in colour, please visit www.stephenrbown.net

Brindle & Glass is pleased to thank the Canada Council for the Arts and the Alberta Foundation for the Arts for their contributions to our publishing program.

Brindle & Glass is committed to protecting the environment and to the responsible use of natural resources. This book is printed on 100% post-consumer recycled and ancient-forest-friendly paper. For more information, please visit www.oldgrowthfree.com.

Brindle & Glass Publishing
www.brindleandglass.com

1 2 3 4 5   10 09 08 07

PRINTED AND BOUND IN CANADA

To Andrew and Clara,
may there always be wild spaces for you to explore

Forgotten Highways

WILDERNESS JOURNEYS DOWN THE HISTORIC TRAILS OF THE CANADIAN ROCKIES

Table of Contents

Map — ix

Introduction: Our Journey — 1

PART ONE: FOLLOWING DAVID THOMPSON

Chapter One: The Mapmaker — 13

Chapter Two: Across the Great Divide — 29

Chapter Three: Valley of the Mammoths — 51

Chapter Four: The Ghosts of the Trade — 67

PART TWO: FOLLOWING SIR GEORGE SIMPSON

Chapter Five: Trail of the Little Emperor — 91

Chapter Six: The Devil's Gap — 103

PART THREE: FOLLOWING CAPTAIN JOHN PALLISER

Chapter Seven: An Irish Sportsman — 123

Chapter Eight: The Mystery of Kananaskis — 139

PART FOUR: FOLLOWING MARY SCHÄFFER

Chapter Nine: Mountain Woman and a Mythical Lake — 159

Chapter Ten: The Abandoned Trail — 173

Epilogue — 191

Further Reading — 194

Acknowledgements — 195

About the Authors — 196

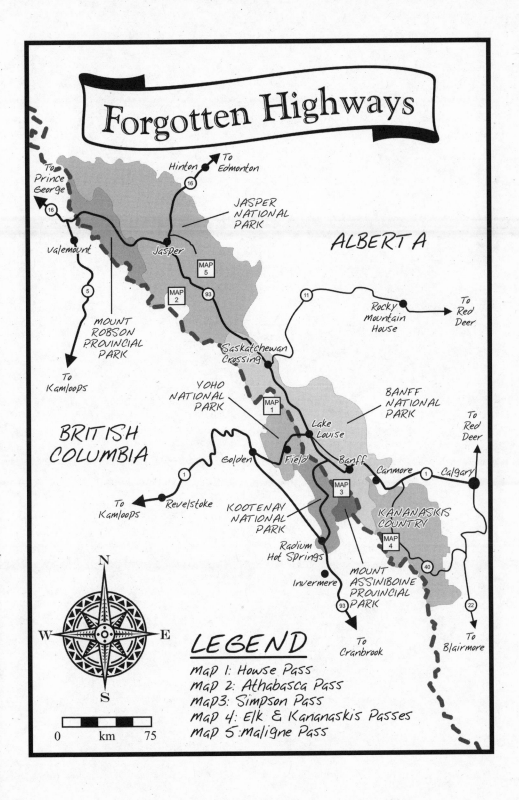

Forgotten Highways

To Prince George

To Edmonton

Hinton

16

JASPER NATIONAL PARK

ALBERTA

Valemount

Jasper

MAP 5

MAP 2

93

5

MOUNT ROBSON P.ROVINCIAL PARK

11

Rocky Mountain House

To Red Deer

To Kamloops

Saskatchewan Crossing

YOHO NATIONAL PARK

BANFF NATIONAL PARK

MAP 1

BRITISH COLUMBIA

Lake Louise

To Red Deer

Golden

Field

Banff

Canmore

1

Calgary

1

Revelstoke

To Kamloops

KOOTENAY NATIONAL PARK

MAP 3

KANANASKIS COUNTRY

MAP 4

Radium Hot Springs

Invermere

MOUNT ASSINIBOINE PROVINCIAL PARK

40

93

22

To Blairmore

To Cranbrook

N

W E

S

LEGEND
Map 1: Howse Pass
Map 2: Athabasca Pass
Map 3: Simpson Pass
Map 4: Elk & Kananaskis Passes
Map 5: Maligne Pass

0   km   75

Introduction
OUR JOURNEY

"There are secrets you will never learn, there are some joys you will never feel, there are heart thrills you can never experience, till, with your horse you leave the world, your recognised world, and plunge into the vast unknown."

Mary Schäffer, Old Indian Trails of the Canadian Rockies, 1907

Steve and I were skiing west, breaking trail on a crisp January day. We followed a clear but narrow path through the pine forest in the bottom of a wide, flat valley near Saskatchewan Crossing. Fresh cougar tracks wound back and forth across the trail—probably from the night before, we convinced ourselves as we struggled up a steep incline of deep snow and emerged onto a windy ridge. We stopped for a snack overlooking the frozen channels of a river that flowed from the head of the valley. Its outlet was hidden from view by the imposing bulk of a mighty ogre-like mountain whose shadow crept over much of the valley. "We could scramble down this hill and just keep on going, it's so flat and open," Steve said. "I wonder where it leads." I looked calmly at him, raising my eyebrows, my breath crystalizing on my hair and hat. It was a look he knew well, and it translated into, "We're not prepared for that kind of trip and you know it, but I won't say so because then I'll seem like the naysayer." What I actually said was, "Let's check the maps and guidebooks and plan a real trip." We later learned that the enticing valley that curved west and south, and headed to a low pass over the Great Divide, was Howse Pass. Canada's first trans-mountain trade route of the fur trade era was established nearly two centuries ago and then shut down because of a violent dispute between rival peoples.

We had only just begun exploring the mountains, having moved to Canmore one year before for its fantastic outdoor recreation opportunities. Steve was quite familiar with the region. He grew up in Calgary and had worked for a few summers for the Alberta Forest Service, but he had been away for many years. Originally from Toronto,

I met Steve while we were both living in St. John's, Newfoundland. He followed me to Vancouver, then I followed him to Ottawa. After a couple of years, we wanted to clear out of the big city to gain easier access to the wilderness. We decided to make the Rocky Mountains home.

In our first summer in the mountains, Steve convinced me to go on a week long backpacking trip. We had tackled shorter journeys before, but I had always been a bit trepidatious about travelling so far off the beaten path for so long. How would I carry all the weight? Would I miss the comforts of home? It turned out to be a great adventure, taking us through some of the premier scenery of the southern Rockies. I was hooked. I loved the feeling of freedom that came from being completely out of touch with everyone and everything I'd ever known (except for Steve, of course). No phone, no email, no watch, no itinerary. Everything we needed to survive was on our backs and we could go anywhere we wanted to go.

Standing on the snowy ridge overlooking the Howse River, Steve had an inkling that a low, flat valley like this must have been important at some time. Steve has always

The flats of the Howse River.

been interested in the history of exploration and knew quite a bit about the explorers who had travelled here. But even he was unsure of the exact routes they had taken through the mountains. And so, our journey to discover Howse Pass began in the library. Throughout the winter, we immersed ourselves in mountain lore and history, something we had overlooked in our celebration of the wilderness. We were a little surprised at what we discovered. These mountains and hills have a long history of human occupation—from early native travellers and traders to the explorers of the fur trade, railway surveyors, mineral prospectors, loggers and finally tourists. This landscape is not, as people sometimes believe, a pristine wilderness untouched by humans that has been preserved for eternity in its original state, primeval and free. I began to appreciate the human presence in the mountain parks, to see how it influenced the development of railroads, highways, and town sites, and how geography had a profound impact on the commercial and political development of the west. When we go hiking or driving through the mountain parks, the routes we travel were not created strictly to facilitate modern pleasure and tourism, but represent a significant part of the history and heritage of this part of the world. On road or foot, we are frequently following in the tracks of people for whom the trails were an integral part of daily life, for travel and trade, hunting and communication.

I read a tantalizingly elusive and vague reference in a magazine about someone who tried to locate the route taken by Captain John Palliser and his surveying expedition of the 1850s. Apparently, it is not entirely clear where he went, and several mountain passes meet the rough description of his proposed route for the railway. How could it be that the route of someone as important to Canadian history as John Palliser remained a mystery? In 1963, *The Beaver* published an article titled "Routes Through the Rockies," by Irene M. Spry, in which the author briefly details the journeys and expeditions of many of the west's early pathfinders. After reading this article, Steve and I unfolded every map of the mountains we had and draped them over the chairs, tables, and floors of our small condo to try to locate the routes of these early adventurers. We were surprised to find that, in many cases, the most significant original travel and trade routes between east and west, or at least portions of them, ran through the various Rocky Mountain national and provincial parks. These routes were still trails, sometimes well over a hundred kilometres long, reasonably untouched by the advances of civilization.

People occasionally hike them for the wilderness experience they provide, but with only a vague knowledge of their historical importance.

The Canadian Rockies are blessed with the largest conglomerate of protected lands on the continent, and rival the greatest parks in the world. The four mountain national parks are a UNESCO World Heritage Site. In addition to the 6,641 square kilometres of Banff, the most famous Canadian national park, the region also hosts Jasper National Park at 10,878 square kilometres, Yoho National Park at 1,310 square kilometres, and Kootenay National Park at 1,406 square kilometres. The several provincial parks that comprise Kananaskis Country in Alberta add thousands more kilometres, not to mention the Whitegoat, Ghost, Wilmore, and Siffleur Wilderness Areas. In British Columbia Mount Robson, Hamber, Height of the Rockies, Assiniboine, and Elk Lakes Provincial Parks help to create a total protected space of more than 30,000 square kilometres, approximately the size of Vancouver Island.

The national parks and some of the provincial parks were created so long ago that they have seen little modern development, other than a handful of luxurious hotels and the busy highways. Many of the backcountry campsites are situated on the same patches of land that hosted native hunters and explorers for thousands of years—a good camping spot then is still a good camping spot now, and for the same reasons. Even in Canada, a country renowned for its wild spaces and low population density, the mountain parks are the closest thing here to true wilderness outside of the subarctic or the far north. Ecological integrity is quite rightfully becoming a prime concern for parks policy as demands for increased development escalate and threaten to destroy the wild character of the region. In spite of the development and several heavily used roads snaking through the heart of the mountains, the mountain parks are still perceived to be "unspoiled" wilderness accessed only by the hundreds of trails that cover thousands of kilometres of the backcountry.

Traversing these trails today is done in much the same manner as it was centuries ago—primarily on foot with heavy packs, with little better defence against mosquitoes or the elements. Although accurate maps are available, and modern technology such as global positioning systems stand as a defence to a complete wilderness experience, in many cases it is as difficult and challenging, or even more so, to cross these mountain passes today, as it was in previous centuries. Routes such as Athabasca Pass are far less travelled today than they were in the golden era of the fur trade. If our society has become so rich that we continually seek out physical and mental challenges in the wilderness—adventure and eco-travel—perhaps it would be a sign of respect to follow at least for a while in the footsteps of those people who in many ways paved the way for our own society and culture and led lives considerably more difficult and uncomfortable than our own. Steve and I began imagining a summer hiking all the significant historical trails to see what we could learn from the early pathfinders about the difficulty of wilderness life and travel. Could we open a window to times past in a land where the terrain has remained essentially unchanged?

Historically, the Rocky Mountains posed a significant barrier to travel, and finding a route through them east or west was not a job for the faint of heart. After nearly one thousand miles of rolling grassland, the Great Plains abruptly end in a seemingly impenetrable wall of forbidding ice-encrusted peaks running the length of the continent from Alaska to Mexico. No one knew what lay beyond the shining mountains, but to taste the brine of the Pacific a route would have to pass over them, not around them. Over hundreds of years, aboriginal peoples, fur traders, European explorers and adventurers, and surveyors all sought to find a safe and easy passage through the craggy defiles of the Rockies.

The first passes through the Rockies were commercial, located and followed by the natives who traded between the east and west sides of the Continental Divide and who hunted in the valleys. Archaeologists have found evidence of human occupation in key mountain valleys dating back more than ten thousand years. Countless thousands of people crossed through these mountains during this time but have left no record of their exploits. In the late eighteenth and early nineteenth centuries the fur traders of the North West Company and Hudson's Bay Company followed in their battle for dominance in the trade. As part of this tectonic realignment of the political order, the Piikani people, known to English-speaking newcomers as the Peigan, drove the Ktunaxa, known as the Kootenay, from the plains west across the Great Divide to the Columbia River valley. Several maps collected by the fur trader Peter Fidler, drawn for him by

Siksika adventurer Old Swan (Ak ko mokki) in 1801, detail some of the trails used by the Siksika people at this time.

As the fur trade waned in the 1850s, political claims to the land became increasingly important. The British needed settlers in the west to bolster and justify their claim to the land, particularly after the loss of the Oregon Territory (the current American states of Oregon and Washington and parts of Idaho and Montana) to the United States in 1846. A government sponsored roadway or railway, they believed, would stand as a bulwark against creeping American encroachment into land they believed was sovereign British, and explorers were sent out to discover the most viable routes. Along with the railway came gentlemen and women of leisure who wanted to explore the mountains and experience the wilderness before the region became corrupted with the taint of civilization, but who ironically contributed to the civilizing process by their very presence.

Our most important criteria for determining the historical routes we would follow was that the trails could be retraced on foot, through wilderness as untamed and lonely as it was in the nineteenth century, allowing us to imagine the struggles and difficulties faced by these early pathfinders. We also wanted to experience the awe they must have felt traversing beneath the ice-clad peaks and stony promontories of this unique region. We were interested in wild and crazy characters such as Scotland's James Carnegie, the Earl of Southesk, who enjoyed an extended hunting expedition in the front ranges in 1858. Lamentably, there wasn't room in our plans for every individual who had blazed a trail in or though the mountains. Nearly every trail in the Rockies has some story behind it. Emphasizing historical significance, because we were limited by time, we still had to choose a small number from a great pool of possibilities. In the end, we settled on five trails that were pioneered by four individuals spanning a time period from 1807 to 1908. The trails we chose would require a least a week to travel and reflected the changing history of the region, from the time of the early fur traders to the arrival of the first of the wealthy adventure-seekers at the beginning of the age of tourism.

David Thompson was the first to push the North West Company's fur trade west across the Continental Divide, over both Howse Pass west of Saskatchewan Crossing and Athabasca Pass leading west from near Jasper to the Columbia River. A seemingly dauntless traveller, originally from England, he spent his formative years, from age fourteen, in the Canadian northwest—beginning at the bleak basin of Hudson Bay, to the great plains, to Great Slave Lake, to the Pacific Ocean. He is Canada's greatest historical geographer. From his retirement home near Montreal, he created a vast and detailed map of western Canada and the northwestern United States.

Forty years later, Sir George Simpson sought a new and possibly safer or less time-consuming route much further south in an attempt to bolster the declining profits of the fur trade. As the undisputed master of the trade, the Little Emperor, as he was known, was a virtual dictator of half a continent. Crafty, vainglorious, and stingy he moulded western Canada during the golden age of Canada's fur trade, creating a complicated logistical network for shipping hundreds of tons of goods around the continent. He died in Montreal in 1860, and his passing coincided with the significant decline of the fur trade.

Captain John Palliser searched for a suitable route for a railway from the prairies into what would later become British Columbia. A great, aristocratic hunter and sportsman, Palliser's expedition began as a glorified hunting trip and ended as a multi-pronged quasi-scientific exploration of much of the southern Rocky Mountains. Because a house fire destroyed most of his personal papers, and his official reports were parcelled out to various British government departments, there is some confusion about his exact routes and recommendations.

Mary Schäffer, a visiting Philadelphia Quaker who fell in love with the Canadian Rockies around the turn of the twentieth century, organized numerous journeys into the backcountry, mostly to satisfy her own curiosity and her love of the wilderness. While a rail line cut through the mountains along the Bow Valley and

Howse Pass National Historic site.

7

west over Kicking Horse Pass, many of the dozens of more remote valleys remained unexplored by non-aboriginal visitors as late as the early twentieth century. Although she may have been among the first to wander down numerous valleys, perhaps her most memorable accomplishment was to blaze a trail to Maligne Lake and Jasper from Laggan Station (Lake Louise) in the south, a route used for decades afterwards. She also lobbied to have the now world-famous Maligne Lake included within Jasper National Park.

As winter turned to spring, Steve and I began planning the wilderness journeys themselves—a time-consuming process even for experienced backpackers. In many cases, the trails we had chosen not only crossed provincial boundaries but passed through several different parks, wilderness areas, and Crown forests with potentially different regulations and policies regarding camping, trail fees, and levels of maintenance. We consulted with officials in all four national parks, many of the surrounding provincial parks, and forestry officials responsible for Crown lands outside park boundaries. From previous backpacking trips we were well aware that, during the course of each trip, segments of the trail could be in starkly different condition—from a smooth well-groomed pathway with bridges over even minor streams, to an overgrown, treacherous, rocky, ill-defined scratch in the dirt where we would be up to our waists fording across medium-sized waterways. In several instances, there was no maintained trail whatsoever, and we would have to bushwhack between segments of trail in surrounding parks. Bushwhacking, the art of travelling cross-country without a trail to follow, is hard work, especially in the more lush and dense forests of British Columbia.

We also had to upgrade our equipment. In the past, I had never cared about the weight of my backpack since Steve is strong as a pack-mule. When I wanted to bring along my latest hard cover novel, he gallantly carried it for me. We were both in good shape and on short trips we could bring along anything we desired—even the occasional cold beer for chilling in a glacial stream. Not so on a seven or eight day journey. We acquired a new tent, lightweight, down sleeping bags, and lightweight, quick-drying and breathable high-tech clothing. We also had to plan a menu that wouldn't break our backs, but would give us enough nutrients and calories to keep us going. And then there was the matter of recording our journey.

Since Steve is a professional writer and popular historian, I left the historical research and writing primarily to him. It was up to me, therefore, to be the chronicler of our adventure. Steve thought I was crazy when I first came home with a Dictaphone, laughing at the idea of a Dictaphone in the wilderness. "How are we going to keep it dry," he asked. "How are we going to keep paper dry," I replied. "We certainly aren't going to remember everything." He soon warmed up to the idea and not far into our first trail was calling out the impressions he wanted me to record. We worked together to record our experiences while we were on the trail. Our thoughts we poured into the Dictaphone and the scenery we captured with a massive pile of archaic and annoyingly heavy camera equipment—tripod and all.

~

The routes of the early explorers often appear in books as dotted lines on a map, without topographic features or elevation, blithely spanning half a continent without any reference to, or recognition of, the difficulty of travel. Living in the Alberta Rockies, and knowing the terrain through which the dotted lines passed, Steve and I understood there was more to the explorers' journeys than what was revealed in the standard oblique references to their accomplishments—"David Thompson, fur trader, 1807," or "Mary Schäffer—Maligne expedition, 1908." There are great stories behind all those dotted lines in the history books, stories of the struggles, hardships, and conquests of the early pathfinders of the North American northwest. By early summer, we were ready to rediscover some of those stories.

Part One
FOLLOWING DAVID THOMPSON

Chapter One
THE MAPMAKER

From a crumbling ridge several kilometres southwest of the Saskatchewan River Crossing in Banff National Park, a deserted wilderness valley, guarded by the brooding sentinels of the Waputik Mountains, heads west and then south toward a cluster of mountains and glaciers at the Continental Divide. The braided channels of the Howse River weave chaotically across the valley floor, surging in volume after the addition of the Glacier Lake Outflow draining the runoff from the Lyell and Mons Icefields. The sparse trees and underbrush make it ideal for horse travel and for keeping your bearings. This valley would lure any adventurer ever deeper into the wilderness.

A rugged trail follows the east shore of the Howse River for about twenty-five kilometres to the base of a rather small forested hill. There is surprisingly little elevation gain to summit this hill, which, remarkably, marks the height of land along the Great Divide. The trail continues, gradually descending into British Columbia following the Blaeberry River. Apart from a brief congested and forested section near the summit, the Blaeberry also flows down a broad and gentle valley of open gravel and sand that descends to the Columbia River near Golden, BC.

The level grade of Howse Pass will come as a surprise to anyone who has seen the wild and impenetrable rock walls and glaciers of the Canadian Rocky Mountains, or driven the treacherous stretch of the Trans-Canada Highway from the Kicking Horse Pass to Golden. Why doesn't the railway or highway follow mellow Howse Pass instead of the circuitous, dangerous, and expensive-to-maintain routes now used?

We asked that same question as we backpacked through Howse Pass, reaching the summit nearly two hundred years after David Thompson and a fur brigade crossed it

Sunset on Glacier Lake.

Flowers along the river flats.

for the first time. It was obvious that we were in a pass; it seemed like a secret gateway through an impenetrable wall to an unknown world on the other side, which of course it was.

Finding a route across the Great Divide was extremely valuable to the fur trade. There are only a handful of viable natural passes through the bewildering maze of peaks and icefields that form the height of land that is now the boundary between Alberta and BC, and locating them was an expensive and uncertain process. These days we hardly notice a good pass, accustomed as we are to the engineering marvels of the twentieth century—highways carved out of rock, bridges spanning frightening torrents, and tunnels shielding the road from avalanches. The internal combustion engine has shrunk the distance between places, and made travel easy, fast, and predictable. On foot, as we were, it became obvious why these original routes were so valuable, why adventurers like David Thompson devoted years to locating them, and why they could become the focal point for simmering political rivalries between the fur-trading companies and tribal hunters and trappers.

David Thompson, Canada's pre-eminent explorer, surveyor, and mapmaker, spent most of his life in the fur trade in North America. Thompson was born in London to Welsh parents in 1770. His father died when he was a small boy of three, and four years later his struggling mother enrolled him in the Grey Coat School of Westminster Abbey, a charity school where he was raised with "piety and virtue . . . [and] a foundation for a sober and Christian life." He was also raised with a basic grounding in Latin, mathematics, geography, and navigation and in 1784, at the age of fourteen, he signed on as an apprentice with the Hudson's Bay Company and departed his native land forever. With the Company, he developed skills as a surveyor and mapmaker and advanced quickly as a trader along the chilly rim of Hudson Bay. But the torpid life of a Bay man was not to his liking. He was a master storyteller, and his *Narrative*, although somewhat embellished from his *Journals*, is a classic of Canadian travel writing. "Neither reading nor writing was required," he later remarked in sour humour, "and my only business was to amuse myself, in winter growling at the cold and in the open season, shooting Gulls, Ducks, Plover and Curlews, and quarrelling with Musketoes and Sand Flies." Thompson was a man of action and the Hudson's Bay Company showed little interest in exploring or surveying the wild terrain under their trading monopoly.

In 1796, with mutual acrimony between himself and the Company, he trudged a hundred and twenty kilometres to the nearest North West Company outpost and offered himself for hire, hoping to explore the vast continent spreading south and west from the isolated huts strung out along the shore of the bay. They offered him the opportunity to combine survey work with fur trading. "How very different the liberal and public spirit of this North West Company of Merchants of Canada from the mean selfish policy of the Hudson's Bay Company styled Honourable," he remarked, pleased with his new circumstances.

Thompson's first assignment for the Nor'Westers was more than he had hoped for: in ten months he was to travel over four thousand miles in almost uncharted country from Lake Superior to Lake Winnipeg, down through Manitoba and Saskatchewan following the length of many of the smaller rivers, to the upper Missouri, and then over to locate the headwaters of the Mississippi. "Every necessary I required [was] to be [put] at my order," he wrote proudly. In the following sixteen years with the North West Company, Thompson roamed over fifty-five thousand miles by canoe, on horseback, and on foot throughout what is now the Canadian west and the American northwest. He slowly compiled journals of thousands of survey notes taken along his many routes, which extended from Hudson Bay in the north, the Missouri River in the south, and

David Thompson taking an observation with a sextant.
C. W. JEFFREYS

the Mississippi River in the east, to the Pacific Ocean in the west. During his wandering years, he would frequently spend several hours every few days observing astronomical phenomena, such as the eclipse of the moons of Jupiter, in order to calculate his latitude and longitude.

When he retired from the trade, he took his thirty years of field survey notes and calculations and created a great map of much of northwestern North America. It was the first chart of the region and was regarded as accurate for more than a century afterwards, securing his reputation as Canada's greatest cartographer and field surveyor. Thompson drew the chart with dark ink on twenty-five separate sheets of rag linen, measuring in full about ten feet wide and six and a half feet tall. The North West Company kept it prominently displayed in the great hall of their most important western base, Fort William on the western shore of Lake Superior, where it could be viewed by anyone travelling to the west.

Thompson is an enigmatic figure, decidedly different from the standard frontier trader. His rugged competence and simple survival instincts were balanced by a sensitive soul and a poetic appreciation for the native cultures and way of life. While his contemporary Simon Fraser was semi-illiterate, acknowledged for his achievements in spite of his cool arrogance, Thompson was a prolific and talented writer eventually producing thirty-nine volumes of journals detailing his roving adventures on the western frontier. He earned a reputation as a fair and honest trader with the native peoples with whom he spent most of his time. On one occasion, "several old Indians made a bargain with me," he noted. "If they should die in winter, I should not demand the debt due to me in the other world—namely, heaven. To which I always agreed."

He also refused to trade liquor after witnessing the devastation it had for native communities, a stubborn act of defiance that earned him the respect of some, but the irritation of others. "I was obliged to take two kegs of alcohol, overruled by my partners," he complained, ". . . who insisted upon alcohol being the most profitable article that could be taken for the Indian trade. . . . When we came to the defiles of the mountains I placed the two kegs of alcohol on a vicious horse, and by noon the kegs were empty and in pieces." He then sent a note to his partners clearly informing them that he would do the same with any other casks of liquor he found in his annual supplies.

Toward his voyageurs, he was less sympathetic. They were more alien to him than the native peoples he respected and emulated. He equally marveled at their simple contentment and disdained their slothful behaviour. "Each man requires eight pounds of meat per day or more," he wrote, astonished. "Upon my reproaching some of them for their gluttony, the reply I got was, 'What pleasure have we in life but eating?' A French Canadian, if left to himself, and living on what he has, will rise very early, make himself a hearty meal, smoke his pipe, and then lie down to sleep again for the rest of the day."

In 1798, at the age of twenty-eight, Thompson married Charlotte Small, the daughter of a wandering trader and a Cree woman, and for the next twenty years they usually travelled together, with their children in tow, across much of the wilderness of northwestern Canada. "My lovely wife is of the blood of these people," he wrote, "speaking their language [Cree] and well educated in the English language, which gives me a great advantage." Although his family members seldom enter into his official journal, one of the few instances they do reveals a bit of Thompson's character. He describes how, on one journey across the mountains, "one of my horses nearly crushing my children to death from his load being badly put on, which I mistook for being vicious; I shot him on the spot and rescued my little ones." Thompson remained loyal to Charlotte and their large family throughout his life—they would have thirteen children together —and, contrary to custom, he brought them east to Montreal when he retired from the trade. Once he wrote to a friend that "it is my wish to give all my children an equal and good education; my conscience obliges it and it is for this I am now working in this country."

Although no official portrait exists of Thompson, according to the physician John Bigsby, who described Thompson in 1820, he "was plainly dressed, quiet and observant. His figure was short and compact, and his black hair was worn long all around, and cut square, as if by one stroke of the shears, just above the eyebrows . . . [He was] friendly and intelligent. . . . Never mind his Bunyan-like face and cropped hair, he has a very powerful mind, and a singular clarity for picture-making. He can create a wilderness and people it with warring savages, so clearly and palpably, that only shut your eyes and you hear the crack of the rifle, or feel the snow-flakes on your cheeks as he talks."

In 1799, the North West Company built a new trading fort on the bank of the North Saskatchewan River, in sight of the Rocky Mountains, and gave it the optimistic name Rocky Mountain House. In September 1800, Thompson moved there as a company clerk. He was to be second in command of an ambitious expedition to cross the mountains and tap the unexploited fur potential of the Far West, an enterprise in tune with his longing to explore new lands. Finding a route through the peaks, rock walls, glaciers, and snaking valleys would be nearly impossible without some knowledge of the region. With no maps, no roads, and no clear idea of the lay of the land, Thompson's only hope, other than educated guessing, was the services of a guide.

He sought the assistance of the Kootenay, originally a Plains tribe that only years before had been pushed west across the mountains by the powerful Peigan, part of the Blackfoot Confederacy that ruled the foothills and western prairie from the Missouri to the North Saskatchewan. Very few Kootenay were willing to venture east of the mountains into the land of the dominant and better armed Peigan. The Peigan profited handsomely as middlemen in the trade and were very careful to keep a monopoly of guns for themselves.

A miniature world alongside the trail.

Three weeks after he had arrived at Rocky Mountain House, Thompson led a delegation into the mountains to meet a band of Kootenay who were venturing east to trade. A suspicious band of Peigan shadowed him the entire journey, and it is a testament to Thompson's diplomacy that he managed to lead the Kootenay, (twenty-seven men, and seven women) back to the fort with only two thirds of their horses stolen. "They are so jealous of the Kootanaes coming in to Trade," Thompson wrote, "that they do all they can to persuade me to return, assuring me that it is impossible for me to find them, and that in endeavouring to search them out, our Horses will fall by Fatigue and Hunger, and perhaps also ourselves." The band of Peigan continued to harass Thompson and the Kootenay, "even to drawing of Arms," to within a few kilometres of Rocky Mountain House. The next day, he traded with the Kootenay for the pelts of wolverines, fishers, bears, and over a hundred beavers. It was an auspicious beginning—the western lands seemed to be rich in furs. Thompson persuaded the Kootenay to send a guide back the following year to lead him west across the Continental Divide.

That winter, Thompson and Duncan McGillivray, the senior partner at the fort, eagerly planned the expedition. The only map they had was from George Vancouver's survey of the coast the previous decade. Although Vancouver was painstakingly accurate, recording the islands and inlets and outline of the coast in great detail, the region between Rocky Mountain House west to the coast remained a vast *terra incognita*. Vancouver's map offered only the vaguest notion of the landmarks described by the Kootenay the previous fall. It did show one key landmark, however, that was a beacon to Thompson— the mouth of a mighty river that poured into the Pacific much further south. It was the Great River of the West, the Columbia, and it was Thompson's ambition to find it and follow it to the Pacific.

With the arrival of spring, Thompson's dreams began to unravel. The long-awaited Kootenay guide was "murdered within a few Miles of the Fort," probably by the Peigan, leaving Thompson without a guide. It was a devastating blow. To make matters worse, McGillivray became ill and gave over leadership of the expedition to James Hughes, the highest ranking trader at Rocky Mountain House. The only other guide who seemed to have any notion of how to cross the mountains was a local Asini Wachi Wininiwak, or Mountain Cree, known as The Rook. He was, according to Thompson, "a Man so Timourous by Nature, of so wavering a Disposition, & withal so addicted to flattering & lying, as to make every Thing he said or did equivocal and doubtful." But without any alternative, Thompson decided against his own instincts to heed the boasts of The Rook.

Thompson's misgivings proved to be well-founded. After bragging about how he had crossed the mountains on a good trail suitable for horse travel, The Rook lead Thompson and the horse brigade up the North Ram River, about fifty kilometres south of the North Saskatchewan. After several weeks of laborious slogging, the valley ended in an impenetrable rock wall: they could go no further. Only then did The Rook sheepishly admit that his claims were false, that not only did he not have horses with him when he ventured into the mountains, but he had never actually crossed the Continental Divide. Thompson was not amused. "Why you Scoundrel," he said, ". . . was it not upon the Supposition that you knew a good Road for Horse across them, that we engaged you for our Guide? Otherwise we would have followed, the best Way we could, the Banks of the Saskatchewan River."

Thompson immediately set out north in the direction of the North Saskatchewan, but the route was exceedingly rocky, treacherous terrain smothered in scraggly close-growing spruce that tore at the horses and equipment. It was weeks later, in early June, that he reached the banks of the North Saskatchewan, several hundred kilometres upstream from Rocky Mountain House. Although Thompson tried to salvage the expedition by building canoes and paddling upriver, as he had seen the Kootenay do the year before, the season was too far advanced—the heat of mid-June had melted the snowpack and glaciers and turned the river into a flooding, silty, raging torrent littered with deadfall. He returned, defeated, to the fort. In a letter to William and Duncan McGillivray, "Agents of the NW Company," Thompson explained his failure and outlined his plans for success the following year. "However unsuccessful this Journey has been," he wrote, "it has not been wholly without its use: it has taught us to make a better choice of our Men, & take fewer of them; & never employ an Indian of this Side of the Mountains for our Guide. . . . Whoever wishes to attempt to cross the Mountains for the Purposes of Commerce ought to employ a Canoe, & start early in the Spring, say the beginning of May, from the Rocky Mountain House, the Water for that Month being low & the current not half so violent as in the Summer. . . . In this Season, they would cross a great Part of the Mountains without extraordinary Difficulty."

Thompson planned to travel up the North Saskatchewan the following season without a guide. But it was not to be. Because of threats to their trading operations in the north, from the Hudson's Bay Company and the newly formed collection of renegade traders united and organized by Alexander Mackenzie called the XY Company, the Nor'Westers set aside plans for expanding the trade, and Thompson spent the next five years in present-day Alberta, Saskatchewan, and Manitoba trading furs. He and Charlotte and their three children only returned to Rocky Mountain House in the fall of 1806, when he was a full partner, to resume his ambitious quest.

The Peigan, however, were no more amenable in 1806 to allowing traders west of their territory than they were in 1801. Hearing of the renewed activity at Rocky Mountain House, the Peigan Chief Kootenae Appee visited the fort on New Year's Day 1807, and again in March, perhaps to warn Thompson against his scheme to venture west. But events conspired to open the route.

The previous summer, two Peigan had been killed in Montana by the Lewis and

Clark expedition. The killings, Thompson wrote, "drew the Peigan to the Missouri to revenge their deaths; and thus gave me an opportunity to cross the Mountains by the defiles of the Saskatchewan River." Thompson was well prepared for his second attempt to push the trade further west. The previous summer, the North West Company had sent several voyageurs, led by Jaco Findlay, up the North Saskatchewan and over the Continental Divide to clear a route for Thompson and the horse brigade. Findlay had met with Thompson during the winter, describing the terrain and drawing a rough map. In early May 1807, under the watchful eyes of the Hudson's Bay Company employees at nearby Acton House, and before the river had become flooded with glacial meltwater, Thompson and his entourage decamped and set off up the North Saskatchewan River. The delegation was an unruly mob that eventually grew to eleven men, five women, and nine children, approximately thirty horses, a pack of yelping dogs, and several canoes. It included Charlotte and their three young children, the youngest a fifteen-month-old bundle strapped to her back.

Thompson pushed ahead on his horse along "a very bad road" to scout the route, and on June 15 noted that "the Snows that have plentifully fallen on the Mountains these three days are now rushing down with such a Noise that we can hardly persuade ourselves it is not Thunder—we hear it at least every Hour, & sometimes oftener." He spent several weeks camped along the Howse River waiting for the snow to melt, and made a short detour to nearby Glacier Lake. He grew bored, and finally, on June 22, he set off up the gravel flats of the Howse River to investigate the snow condition toward the pass. He was astonished to find it clear: "in all probability there is no snow to stop us in the rest of our Road." He immediately sent word to bring up the sprawling cavalcade. The ascent to the pass was relatively easy, consisting mostly of wandering the gravel flats and then ascending a small wooded hill to a "meadow full of springs at the foot of the surrounding Mountains, forming a hollow—not to be noticed at any distance."

The route down the other side, along today's Blaeberry River, proved another matter. The trail that Thompson had ordered to be marked the previous fall by two Nor'Westers, in anticipation of the crossing, was totally useless for a heavily laden horse brigade. "From what has been said of the Road on the Portage, it is clearly seen that Jaco Findlay with Men engaged last Summer to clear the Portage Road, has done a mere

Looking back toward Saskatchewan crossing.

nothing," Thompson wrote in frustration. "The Road was nowhere cleared any more than just to permit Jaco & his Family to squeeze thro' it with their light baggage and it is the opinion of every man with me, as well as mine, that Jaco ought to lose at least half his wages for having so neglected the Duty for which he was so expressly engaged."

The pack train wound precariously down through the overgrown, tangled morass, crossing and recrossing the torrential river wildly swollen above its banks in the heat of late June. "The Trees every where fallen down & the Moss overgrown with a kind of wild willow vine & very sharp prickly Shrubs—we had to cut much wood away & widen the Path. Add to this, the Horses were obliged to jump with their Loads over much wind-fallen Wood . . . The Men had much ado to save themselves." The trees grew so close together and congested along the shore of the river that they had to search for the sporadic flat portions and continually cross the wild water to get back and forth to them. "We crossed and recrossed every hundred Yards," Thompson related, "the Stream winding continually from the foot of one Hill to the foot of the other, besides sending off many channels. . . . The Current is so very rapid & deep, that I often expected to see the Men & Horses with their loads swept away before it, but thank God all got safe hereto, tho' much wilted." Slowed by the tremendous quantities of deadfall and the deadly river crossings, it took five days to descend the sixty kilometres to the Columbia River (despite the relatively clear flats along the lower Blaeberry). On June 30, the weary train of adventurers emerged from the narrow defiles of the Blaeberry Valley into a grassy clearing in a broad north–south valley with a great river lazily winding its way north. Thompson called the river the Kootenay (in reality, it was the Columbia but he wouldn't realize this until years later).

They descended into the verdant valley of the upper Columbia, free of the congesting alders, willows, and devil's club along the Blaeberry, and into a drier, open land of pines and clearings. Despite his adventurous disposition, Thompson was always a pragmatic man and a good fur trader. Building a small fort as a base was his first priority, although he longed to continue exploring. "I found myself necessitated to leave aside all thoughts of discovery for the present and bend my whole aim to an establishment for trade . . . and as our pressing necessities did not allow time for thought upon thought, I set out to look for a place where we might build, that . . . I might be at liberty to seize every opportunity of extending my knowledge of the country." A band of Kootenay warned Thompson that his first site for a fort was too distant from fresh water and was not sufficiently defendable from attack. Thompson's troops moved further south to a fine site along Toby Creek and founded Kootenae House trading fort just north of Lake Windermere. It was strongly built with stockade walls protecting the log houses, one side "resting on the steep bank of the River . . . the stockades were all ball proof, as well as the Logs of the Houses." Thompson wanted to be ready in case the Peigan attacked.

They settled into a domestic–nomadic life, tramping over the brownish dry hills, following rivers through much of interior British Columbia, western Montana, Idaho, and Washington, and inviting the tribal hunters and their families to trade at the post. Although Thompson made several attempts to locate the elusive Great River of the West, his time was consumed building the fur trading network in the new Columbia Division and collecting astronomical observations for his great chart. Trade from the Columbia Division doubled each year for the next four years and additional trading posts were constructed—Kullyspell House and Saleesh House in Idaho and western Montana. The North West Company developed a network of affiliations and alliances with the many local peoples and pushed the trading frontier not only west, but also north and south. Each fall about one thousand kilograms of goods passed west over Howse Pass, and each spring thousands of furs returned east. It was becoming a well-travelled and well-known route. But the golden era of the fur trade through Howse Pass was about to end.

In the late winter, early in 1810, Finan McDonald was hunting as the guest of a Saleesh band when the group was surprised by a band of Peigan. It was not a peaceful encounter and during the battle seven Peigan and five Saleesh were killed. The Saleesh were armed with guns supplied by the North West Company and two of the Peigan may have been killed by McDonald himself. Long irritated with the trade that was undermining their role as middlemen, annoyed and perhaps afraid that their enemies were acquiring guns, and humiliated by an unparalleled military defeat, the Peigan moved to shut down Howse Pass.

Thompson had ventured east of the mountains in the spring of 1810, perhaps for a brief holiday, and when he set out to return through Howse Pass in the fall, Kootenae Appee and a well armed war band lay in ambush near Shunda Creek, upstream from Rocky Mountain House. They waylaid the annual canoe brigade as it paddled up the North Saskatchewan River and forced them, and the entire annual complement of supplies destined for the far side of the Continental Divide, to return under guard to Rocky Mountain House. There was no violence, but neither was there a peaceful way to bypass the Peigan blockade. A few months earlier a Hudson's Bay Company spy named Joseph Howse had crossed the pass and was turned around by the Peigan with a stern warning not to cross again. "If they ever again met with a white Man going to supply their Enemies," Howse wrote, "they would not only plunder and kill him, but they would make dry Meat of his body." Although the pass was later named after him, Joseph Howse quickly returned east and never crossed the Continental Divide again.

Thompson had been waiting upstream from the blockade for his canoe brigade, and so for several weeks did not know they had been escorted back to Rocky Mountain House. When he did hear the news from one of his lieutenants, he was not surprised. News of the battle between the Peigan and the Saleesh had not yet reached the Nor'Westers, but Thompson had no doubt of the reasons for the aggressive blockade. Rather than engaging in a gun battle with his customers, Thompson regrouped as quickly as possible and led the brigade on a harrowing and uncertain overland journey north, through the

Postage stamp commemorating Thompson's travels.

uncharted wilds of the front ranges of what is today Jasper National Park, searching
for an alternate pass west to the Columbia. The history of Howse Pass, unaccountably
named after a man who crossed it only once, during the last year of its use, drew to a
close.

The forest repossessed the trail where hundreds of horses had trod. Creeping
undergrowth reclaimed the semi-permanent camps. Howse Pass became deserted; all the
scars and markings of the busy trade and travel erased. Even the Kootenay did not need
the pass anymore because the North West Company found a new trade route. Today
the David Thompson Highway in Alberta heads from the abandoned site of Rocky
Mountain House, now a National Historic Site, west to where it intersects the Icefields
Parkway near the junction of the North Saskatchewan and Howse Rivers in Banff
National Park. The park maintains several trails in the region, roughly approximating
the original trail. On horseback, much of the route west and south from the highway
to the summit of Howse Pass can be easily covered by plodding up the gravel flats of

the valley bottom. The David Thompson Heritage Trail, maintained by the BC Forest Service, descends from the pass along the Blaeberry River until it connects with a logging road from Golden. It is all wilderness and, on a map at least, a trip here looks to be quite an adventure. There are many other trails in the national parks with more spectacular scenery or better-maintained infrastructure and conditions, but not many with the same historical pedigree—a place where significant events transpired, where imagination adds to the mix of solitude and challenge. Like Thompson nearly two centuries earlier, by late June we could not wait any longer for the snow to melt.

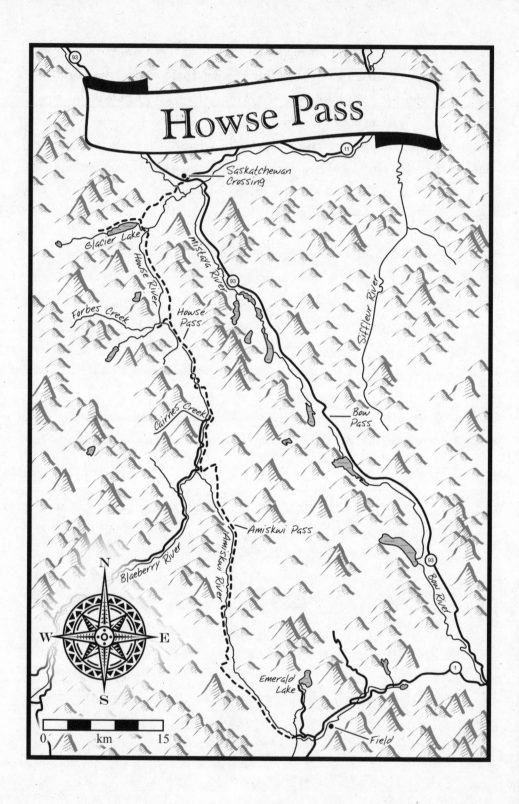

Chapter Two
ACROSS THE GREAT DIVIDE

rue to fur trade tradition, we got a Hudson's Bay Company start to our first trip. We were late. It was afternoon by the time we had loaded our small red Mazda pick-up truck, checked everything for the fourth time, wound our way through the congested summer traffic of downtown Canmore, and headed west on the Trans-Canada Highway. The fur brigades during the golden era of the trade deliberately started late on the first day of an expedition, but for a more practical reason than our own chronic tardiness—after setting up camp on the first night, they would still be close enough to the fort to send someone back if they had forgotten something.

In our day and age, unfortunately, this wasn't such a practical solution. Our time is measured in hours and days, not weeks and months. If we forgot anything we would have to do without, because with only seven or eight days to complete the trip, with the national parks requiring a daily itinerary, and with our own somewhat inflexible schedule, the margin for error was slim. Nor could we bail out of the trip if the weather turned sour. In this way, I fancied our own logistical problems to be different from, but on par with Thompson's. While he was forced to wait for favourable conditions, for the moment when the snow had melted but before the rivers flooded, we were forced to push on to keep up with our own pre-arranged itinerary.

We drove two separate vehicles along the congested pre-long-weekend highway; Steve drove our silver Toyota Tercel, ten years old and still chugging uphill, and I drove our truck. We planned to leave the truck at the end of the trail near Field, BC, where we hoped to emerge a week later. Anxious to get away from the road and into the backcountry, we pulled off the highway into Lake Louise to register with Parks Canada. The guidebooks suggested that Howse Pass was a depressing, viewless slog over rooty and marshy flats, definitely not worth the effort of hiking. So we were pleased when one of the park interpreters told us that, although it was rugged, it was a peaceful and beautiful valley, perfect for solitude.

I told him we planned to continue on over the pass into BC, to follow David Thompson's 1807 journey. There was a moment of silence. "They don't maintain the trail much in BC," he said, looking at the map. "The only people who head that way are the wardens, the trail crew . . . and you."

As for fording the Howse River, he blithely informed us that we "might get swept away." I think he was joking. Then he said that we should "try walking along the shore until you find a shallower area if the official ford looks dangerous." Oh great, I thought, as I left. Just what we need: a deserted valley with a poor trail and a river ford running dangerously high because the suddenly hot weather was melting the snow pack.

I dropped off our truck at the Natural Bridge near Field, and then got into the car with Steve. We retraced our route, turning north on the Icefields Parkway to get to Saskatchewan Crossing. The Parkway is a winding two lane road that parallels the Great Divide as it heads north following the Bow River past a series of blue, teardrop glacial lakes, including the headwaters of the Bow. Periodically, the road crested a hill, giving us a glorious panorama of forest lined valleys beneath ominous and rugged snow-dappled peaks that form an endless wall of rock and ice, impenetrable as far north as Saskatchewan Crossing and the entrance to Howse Pass. There are no towns along the Parkway, and in the winter the road is often in poor condition, with a somewhat ominous sign that states "Warning, no gas for 230 KM."

After about two hours, and several hundred kilometres of vehicle travel, we approached Saskatchewan Crossing. Named after the river ford, it was now a giant parking lot surrounded by flimsy-looking bungalows, a commercial visitor centre that serves overpriced greasy food, and a gift store that sells mountain souvenirs. "If David Thompson had known that the place where he camped and watched bison wandering in the valley would be smothered in this sprawling congestion less than two hundred years later," Steve said, "he might have kept the route a secret." I looked over and realized he was only half-joking. "That's just your own fantasy," I said. ""It's impossible to know what any early explorer would have thought." I had to concede that this amount of development, this number of vehicles roaring by on broad permanent roads, would have been inconceivable in those quiet, slower times. A road in Thompson's era meant a rugged track that serviced a few dozen humans, fifty horses, and a pack of dogs several times a year.

We had allocated seven days of hiking to complete the trip, and after we hoisted our packs in the parking lot just north of Saskatchewan Crossing, we were suitably impressed when we visually traced our upcoming route on our map. We were not following the highway, but taking the back route to Field, on foot, a distance of 110 to 120 kilometres. "Do you realize that we have just driven, in two hours, a greater distance than we are about to walk in the next week?" I said. Steve looked thoughtful, but had nothing to say.

On that deflating note, we set off into the woods, a scraggly canopy of lodgepole pine. In 1807, Thompson and his entourage rode their horses up the river flats and then camped, waiting for the weather to warm and the snow to melt, making a side trip to explore Glacier Lake. We decided to follow the official trail directly to Glacier Lake, and then descend to the valley bottom, ford the Howse River, and continue along its eastern shore the following day. Because we were on foot and not horseback, this was the only

Glacier Lake.

feasible route to take in both Howse Pass and the lake that James Hector named fifty years later after reading Thompson's account. It was a rolling ten kilometre trail to the lake, part of it through the regenerating remnants of Banff's last large natural forest fire that swept the valley in 1940.

After a brief climb over the crest of an adjacent valley, we emerged at the shore of a sparkling oval lake surrounded by steep mountains. At the far shore arose a great rock wall with a glacier oozing down from an icefield that lay further to the west along the height of land. Rivulets of dirty ice and snow streamed down the wall of the mountains at the end of the lake, and terrible swaths of mangled trees marked avalanche chutes on the surrounding mountainsides. We gratefully heaved our twenty to thirty kilogram packs to the ground (Steve's being the heavier one, of course) and set up camp in the woods near a gravelly patch of shore. After the tent was up, the thermarests and sleeping bags tossed in and unravelled, we each went about our usual tasks. I rummaged through our food bag and set up the stove, while Steve filtered drinking water from the lake. While eating our dinner of rehydrated dehydrated maple beans and a cup of tea, we watched the sky turn pink as the last of the dark clouds blew away and the sun illuminated the caps of the towering peaks and the shimmering glacier. Our thoughts turned to David Thompson, who, according to his *Journals,* enjoyed the same scene on "a fine day" with "flying clouds" on June 9, 1807. Before it was fully dark, we hoisted our great sack of provisions into the air—and out of reach of bears and squirrels—on the cable and pulley system provided by Parks Canada.

It was a restless night. First nights on the trail are often unsettled, as many backwoods travellers will confirm. It takes time for the body to adjust to new rhythms, sounds, and smells and to accommodate the annoying lumps from roots and rocks protruding through a thin sleeping mat. I was tossing and turning on the uneven ground. After a few minutes, Steve muttered, "I was thinking of putting a pea under your mattress." It took me a while to figure out what he was talking about, and by then he was asleep.

In the morning, after a quick breakfast, we packed up and set off on a side trail that led down from Glacier Lake to the Howse Valley, where we hoped to ford the river and connect to the trail, on the southeast side, which led west and south toward the pass. Before crossing Glacier Lake Outflow, the prosaically named waterway that drains the lake into the Howse River, we came to a vantage point overlooking the valley, and it was here that we saw the pass spreading out beneath us. Just as it was two hundred years ago, the valley was a chute carved from the surrounding mountains, worn flat from centuries upon centuries of meltwater rushing from the icefields and glaciers along the Continental Divide. The Howse River here spreads out across the entire valley bottom, braided and contorted into half a dozen or so smaller channels, making it possible to ford without getting swept away. Just before we reached the Glacier Lake Outflow, Steve spied a mottled brown grouse walking slowly in the shadows from the forest. Six soft yellow and black chicks emerged from the bush making chirping noises as they followed their mother down the path. We remained still until they had passed into the bush. In another era, we would have eaten them for dinner.

The Glacier Lake Outflow, the first of several anticipated fords, looked deep and formidable. We changed into sandals and unstrapped the waist belts of our packs, so that if we lost our footing we could disentangle ourselves from our packs. I had never forded a river and wondered exactly what type of adventure I had agreed to participate in. But with Steve in the lead, looking solid and secure, I waded into the current. At

Steve battling the current.

midstream, it was up to my thighs. I made it across, heart racing but safe, and we began picking our way across the flood plain, crossing several smaller streams before coming upon the main channel of the Howse River. The water was becoming brown, silty, and swollen in the midday heat, preventing us from seeing the bottom to judge the depth. Great standing waves foamed from the turbulence caused by hidden rocks. Steve, taller at six feet compared to my five feet eight inches, stronger and heavier, went first. It was a slow and somewhat frightening crossing, as he slid forward in the murky, freezing, and fast flowing water with only a hiking pole for balance. He was silent and intently focused on the waves in front of him. I entered when he was midstream. The white water surged up to soak the bottom of my pack and on several occasions we both stopped, rigid, and straining against the current to regain our balance. At one point my downstream foot was nearly swept out from under me and I had to struggle to bring it back against the flow. Once we began, however, there was no turning back, the current was too swift and deep. To turn around and face either upstream or downstream would have meant going for a swim. My focus on survival was so intense, I only noticed the frigid cold of the glacial water when I emerged, shaking from the adrenaline and physical effort, into the sun on the far bank.

When I first met Steve in St. John's and he told me history was one of his greatest interests, I couldn't imagine anything more boring. I certainly never pictured myself struggling through a raging torrent in the middle of nowhere on the trail of David Thompson. I sure wasn't bored—exhausted, frightened maybe, but also exhilarated. I'll never forget the experience.

After clambering from the stagnant almost swampy water at the fringe of the final channel, we climbed up a nearby embankment and collapsed, exhausted, on an open hillside. We took off our wet clothes, set them out to dry, and put on our only other dry shorts and T-shirts. We then relaxed and ate a snack of nuts and dried fruit to regain strength. The fording left me far more drained than I had expected. Now, from experience, I knew why Thompson recommended travel in the spring and fall only—the water is too much of an obstacle in the summer. We rested in the warmth of the sun for half an hour, studying the map and guessing where the official Parks Canada trail lay, behind us in the forest somewhere. Across the river we could see the valley and glacier we had come from that morning. Birds were chirping, butterflies and other insects were hovering about, and several eagles soared above the flats, circling ever higher in the wind currents. The surrounding mountains were muscular, rocky, and forbidding. From our vantage, we could see that the high flood marks of the Howse River were considerably higher than the current water level; another few days of hot weather and I never could have forded the river here.

After thrashing through the woods for about five hundred metres, we intersected the trail and began hiking through the forest up the valley, with fifteen kilometres to go to reach what looked like a good place to camp. The valley seemed like a broad and flat flood plain that snaked around several mountains and wound its way ever deeper into the depths of the Rockies. The trail was covered in deadfall that we had to climb over, balancing the weight of our packs while avoiding as much as possible muddy or swampy sections left from the recent rains. A continuous series of spider webs blocked our path, a sure indication that no one had preceded us down this route for a few days at least, and spiny juniper bushes crept onto the trail, scraping at our legs. Not very graciously, I let Steve take the lead. We saw no other boot marks.

Like most people, knowing where I am and how to get to where I want to go is something I take for granted. In the backcountry, even with detailed maps and a global positioning system, I never know exactly where I am. More precisely, despite having a fairly good idea of where I am according to the map, I never know what lies between me and my destination. The trail might deteriorate, the river might be flooded, a bear might block the path. Our packs contained less gear and supplies than those of earlier travellers; but we were on foot, not horses, so we probably covered country at about the same speed. Walking gives a very different perspective than driving the same distance. At a hundred kilometres per hour, I see a mountain and then quickly move on to the next one, constantly bombarded by new sights and vistas. During the three days it took us to trudge up to the height of land, we observed the same set of mountains, sometimes in early morning light, sometimes in the setting sun, always from a slowly changing perspective or angle. By the time we reached the pass, and were treated to a new vista, I felt like I knew those mountains intimately.

The twenty kilometre trek from Glacier Lake was grueling and long and at last we found a good flat patch of land on which to camp, near the headwaters of the Howse River. There were no official sites here, so we selected a sheltered spot and set up our

tent on the brushy flats of Conway Creek, near the unoccupied Howse Valley Warden Station. Good camping spots are hard to come by and here we had a great view, were sheltered from the wind, close to a water source, and on level ground. Judging by the absence of boot tracks in the dirt, we were the only people in the Howse Valley. We had total peace, hearing only the wind as it caressed hundreds of square kilometres of evergreen trees, and the burbling of the creek full of glacial runoff. We celebrated Canada Day in the solitude of true wilderness. Even though Banff National Park and the surrounding parks were undoubtedly crowded on a hot summer long weekend, the roads plugged with RVs, the town of Banff bursting with tourists, every hotel filled to capacity, every tee time booked on every golf course, and every front country campground and the popular backcountry sites booked, we didn't have to travel that far to the avoid crowds completely. A vast amount of space in the parks remains wild, as it should, even during crowded holidays. You just have to be willing to walk for twenty kilometres or so to get there.

After eating a hasty meal of homemade beef jerky and crackers and hanging our food from the branch of a large aspen tree, we wandered to the freezing creek and washed the sweat from our faces and necks and went to bed early for a night of sound sleep. We had planned the next day as a rest day of sorts, our only goals to explore the headwaters of the Howse River, take some photographs, and record our thoughts. Steve believed the area had some historical significance, and he wanted to imagine the events of the past. This was the final bit of open, flat ground before the forest covered hill at the crest of Howse Pass. When Thompson and his entourage first crossed the pass in 1807, they followed the flats the entire distance up the curving Howse Valley and likely passed through this same clearing where we were now camped. For years before 1807, the Kootenay used the pass to come east and trade at what is now called Kootenay Plains, and for three years after, the fur traders of the North West Company all probably camped in this very spot as they passed west.

We spent a relaxed day along Conway Creek, keeping our same camp and making several short excursions to inspect the most likely locations of Thompson's travels. At the confluence of several small tributaries to the Howse River, I could see all the way down

The overgrown trail.

the valley to the mountains at Saskatchewan Crossing. Our map indicated that one of the looming mountains was named Mount David, presumably after David Thompson. It was large and impressive, but not eye-catching. It was robust around the bottom but with only a little peak barely noticeable from our camp—somehow dwarfed by the surrounding spires and glaciers. Steve thought it fitting that Mount David, formidable yet lacking the rugged flourishes of the surrounding peaks, mirrored precisely Thompson's own position as a somewhat unrecognized pioneer and traveller in Canadian history. Despite his undeniable accomplishments, he is somehow overshadowed by other more flamboyant pathfinders, such as Alexander Mackenzie or Simon Fraser.

On July 2, we awoke to a layer of frost covering our tent, and spent a slow morning reluctantly packing for the next leg of our journey—eighty to eighty-five kilometres over the next four days. My shoulders were still sore and I wasn't looking forward to being "saddled" with my pack again. Despite the early chill, it was a beautiful morning and we lingered over our delicious and hearty breakfast of Prairie Cherry Oatmeal before setting off. It soon became hot under the clear skies and we slipped into a good hiking rhythm. Without really gaining much elevation, we quickly covered the three kilometres to the summit of the pass and found ourselves in a clearing in an alpine region, with spongy ground and scraggly stunted trees, occasionally smothered in snow mould. Near us was a provincial boundary marker, beside a Heritage Canada Plaque, while on the other side of the clearing was a primitive wood sign informing us that this was the first trade route to the west, and that David Thompson had passed this way on June 25,

At the summit of Howse Pass.

1807—almost two hundred years before us. I stopped, looked at Steve, and said, "A bit anti-climactic, eh?" He nodded in agreement. "Not very scenically impressive, is it, for such an important place."

It was here that our camera seized in mid-photo and refused to work for the remainder of the trip. Now we truly felt like idiots. Not only were we carrying seven kilograms of photography equipment, but now the camera didn't work. We did manage to capture one image of us standing beside the sign. Resisting the temptation to curse the camera gods, we shrugged, settled into a philosophical silence, and continued through the pass into what is now BC. After a while, the trail became sketchy and ill-defined and seemed to skirt the edges of several small lakes or ponds until it finally vanished in a large marshy clearing several kilometres from the boundary, probably the same clearing where Thompson camped on his first crossing of Howse Pass. I found one set of prints, Steve another, left by a moose and by a large grizzly, neither of which we wanted to follow. Steve consulted our three maps, while I searched through our guidebooks. The 1985 Parks Canada map showed a trail clearly following the east side of the Blaeberry River, which had its headwaters not far from where we were standing. The Gem Trek

Where the trail disappeared . . .

map, usually the most trustworthy, showed the trail following the west side of the river, while the National Topographic Series map, supposedly unreliable for trail locations, showed a trail vaguely summiting a hill adjacent to the river and coming down again near the Lambe Glacier outflow three or four kilometres downriver. The guidebooks were all clear on one thing: that a trail of some sort was somewhere.

We tried the hill trail first because Steve observed an ill-defined but worn looking path heading almost in that direction. But after thrashing about in dense alder thickets through burned over land that was now covered in scraggly spruce, we abandoned that plan and descended the hill to the steep v-shaped gorge that funneled the Blaeberry south and west toward the Columbia River. We found no trail on either side of the Blaeberry, here at its headwaters only a small stream, but we pushed on in the hope a trail would emerge. I know now why Thompson was so angry with Jaco Findlay who failed to clear a good track through these bushes. It seems to become easily overgrown. The conditions were made worse by the old clear-cut we had entered as soon as we had crossed into BC. The new growth had yet to mature and the ground was covered with brambles and other spiny and tangled weeds, as well as skeletal burned trees thrusting from the chaotic detritus like sentinels.

I was seriously doubting the bold promises in one of our guidebooks that a "good trail continues across the pass and onto the headwaters of British Columbia's Blaeberry River. The track passes through meadows and beside small pools before descending to an aluminum bridge over Lambe Creek, just below a small waterfall."

If there was a trail, we somehow failed to find it—certainly there wasn't a good trail. Every footstep was blocked. We clambered over rocks, thrashed through a wall of sinewy willows and clusters of tangled alders that sprouted from the rocky earth like wrist-thick tentacles. Steve pushed and grunted his way through, much like a bear, while I was more delicate, trying to pick my way between the tangled thicket. Finally we decided to wade down the centre of the stream, but it too was plugged with rotting and burned logs. I'm not allowed to print what Steve had to say about this. Colourful, to be sure, but it would also take several pages. Far to the southwest, I could see the Lambe Glacier, and I knew that we had to cross its outflow stream, undoubtedly swollen with silty meltwater, but theoretically blessed with a permanent aluminum bridge. I began to wonder whether the bridge existed, but quickly banished the thought—bad for morale.

I did not want to admit defeat and turn back, so pushed on. It was impossible to get lost—the Blaeberry ran down the bottom of a narrow valley.

Unfortunately, the terrain was not flat and we were still more than ten kilometres from our camp. As the river was flooding over its banks and hemmed in by cliffs, we were forced to go up and over the hills through the dense forest, dragging ourselves up the inclines. Dead branches broke and crumbled in our hands as we sought leverage on steep hills. Living branches were frequently covered in thorns or spikes. We crested rocky outcroppings, scrambled along the edge of boulder strewn rock slides, and descended to innumerable small streams, struggling up and down their banks. I wished I had a machete to hack through the wild scrub. I was exhausted and covered in dirt and evergreen needles, sweating in the thirty degree heat. Bloody scratches covered my arms and legs where the underbrush had scraped the skin and thorns had pricked me. Steve was no better off. Finally, after five hours of the hardest, most frustrating hiking either of us had ever done, we clawed up an embankment and suddenly burst into a small clearing. We had, at last, stumbled upon a trail.

After a short rest, Steve couldn't resist the temptation of following the trail back the way we had come to see where it went. We would have cursed ourselves if we had somehow missed the trail.

"I'll guard the packs," I offered, glad to sit for a while longer. "After all, I wouldn't want a bear to get our food."

"Yeah, that would truly make this my most memorable day on the trail," Steve observed dryly.

Fortunately for our own pride, Steve reported that the trail ended in a sprawling swamp with grasses and horsetail sprouting from the muck. No footprints—human, moose, deer, or bear—entered or exited the stinking quagmire, and he could see no trail continuing on the other side.

We strolled easily to the outflow stream and were immensely relieved to discover that there was an oddly out-of-place, substantial aluminum bridge over the raging torrent. A beautiful waterfall surged over a rocky cliff upstream. We crossed the bridge and continued down the valley, stepping over mounds of fresh horse droppings. Although it was getting late, we had several kilometres to go to reach our planned camp. I later calculated that we had travelled only three kilometres in five hours of bushwhacking—

A welcome sight after hours of bushwhacking.

perhaps a record for slow travel. Further down the trail, Steve spied a cheery aluminum trail sign from the BC Forest Service proclaiming that we were on the David Thompson Heritage Trail.

Before staggering into camp at around 8:30 PM, at the base of the appropriately named Doubt Hill, we encountered one final obstacle—an evil-looking, rumbling torrent innocently named Cairns Creek. Although only a tiny blue line on our map, the thought of wading across it was almost as frightening to me as the prospect of retracing our route to the pass. Fortunately, a little upstream Steve saw a huge tree bridging the treacherous channel and we crossed to safety, finally reaching the Cairns Creek Forest Recreation Site, a primitive campground maintained by the BC Forest Service, which could be reached by rough logging road from the Columbia Valley near Golden. The camp was deserted, although a scrawled note in the register indicated that the previous night it was populated with "5 people, 7 horses, 2 bears and 1 rabbit." We didn't care to meet the bears so, despite our exhaustion, we spent forty-five minutes scouting for a good branch from which to hang our food. A sign at the camp helpfully suggested we store it in the trunk of our car.

The morning of our fourth day was again clear and sunny and already showed signs of considerable heat. We awoke late and, with creaky bones and muscles, made a slow departure from camp along a logging road that followed the Blaeberry River southwest, and rapidly descended in elevation. From here we could have continued on old logging roads, in our truck or mountain bikes if we had them, all the way to the Columbia Valley just north of Golden, but we had decided instead to branch southeast over Amiskwi Pass and follow the Amiskwi River to Field, in Yoho National Park. This too was an

The flats of the Blaeberry River.

historic route, pioneered by the Kootenay in the late eighteenth century. These prairie peoples were driven west into and across the mountains by their aggressive rivals the Peigan soon after the introduction of the horse onto the prairies in the late 1700s. They frequently travelled east over Amiskwi Pass and Howse Pass to the Kootenay Plains until as late as the second half of the nineteenth century, when the railroad over the treacherous Kicking Horse Pass was completed. At Kootenay Plains, they traded ochre and furs with other plains peoples and fur traders and hunted for bison and other game. When Thompson headed west, he was following an established route in use for decades before the North West Company sought to expand the fur trade west of the Rockies.

After about ten kilometres of walking down the logging road in the baking sun, we came upon a large bridge crossing the Blaeberry River, which by this time had evolved from a meandering brook into a silty torrent perhaps forty feet wide and impossible to ford. Further west, where it surges into the Columbia, the Blaeberry doubles again in size and is a popular canoeing spot. After dousing ourselves in the blessedly cold waters, we set off south and up along an abandoned logging road. It was a blisteringly hot day without shade as we trudged ever upward through burned clear-cut land for an additional seventeen kilometres and about one thousand metres of elevation gain.

Late in the afternoon, we had ascended on switchbacks high enough to clearly see the Mummery Glacier to the north plugging the valley like a massive ice wall, a great blue and white glob slowly drooping from its lofty plateau. The rock was streaming wet from the sunny melt, and speckled and contoured with snow. Great gouges and chutes marked the progress of rock slides and avalanches. Looking back the way we had come, I was astonished to see the low forested hill of Howse Pass, dwarfed by monumental rock crags along the Great Divide. I spied Mount David, rounded and grey, beneath which we had camped two days before, and perhaps even the mountains, in the distance, of Saskatchewan Crossing. From this vantage, near Amiskwi Pass, Howse Pass looked so obvious as the easiest path through the bewildering maze of valleys and peaks.

But for historical accident, the Howse Valley might well have become the route of the railway in the late nineteenth century. If not for Chief Kootenae Appee and the Peigan blockade, it would have remained the primary route across the mountains, instead of falling into disrepair and becoming so overgrown that when James Hector of the Palliser expedition searched for it in 1859, he could scarcely find a trace of the early trail.

The railway surveyor James Moberly recommended this route for the railroad but well-connected investors and executives had already speculated on land further south, around Calgary. They were anxious to push a route that would make them money, saddling unsuspecting future generations of taxpayers with hundreds of millions of dollars in expenses, subsidizing railway and road construction through the Kicking Horse Pass route. Howse Pass would have made an admirable route compared to the Kicking Horse Pass, which after numerous train wrecks and dozens of fatalities required the construction of outrageously expensive spiral tunnels bored from the interior of two nearby mountains to decrease the grade. The railway could have followed the Howse River to its headwaters and then descended adjacent the Blaeberry to the Columbia Valley.

The highway would then have followed the rail line, and Glacier Lake, instead of Lake Louise, would be adorned with an elegant château. If not for current Parks Canada policy that strives to maintain wilderness and disallows additional road construction within the park boundaries, Howse Pass might still become a well-used highway. Politicians in Red Deer, AB, frequently raise the issue of a road from Saskatchewan Crossing to Golden, BC. Many businesses are eager for a drastic reduction in the time it takes to transport goods between central Alberta and the British Columbia coast. Despite the route's obvious practicality, anyone interested in wilderness or historical conservation would consider a road through this mostly untouched valley a disaster. Howse Pass is nearly as peaceful and wild as it was during Thompson's day and, hopefully, is likely to remain that way—though in Steve's opinion more hikers should make the trek to the crest of the pass, a National Historic Site, and appreciate the cultural and historical significance of Canada's first large-scale cross-mountain trade route. If we don't appreciate it and savour it, our past will be lost. Not every hike needs to lead into the high alpine or the most beautiful terrain. There are other reasons for selecting hiking destinations, and honouring the people of the past is one of them.

After enjoying the panoramic view of Howse Pass, we continued on up the road as it now turned south toward Amiskwi Pass and Yoho National Park. I was so tired that Steve practically had to drag me to get me started. He refused outright to stop and camp here beside the road. Thankfully, the last few kilometres were reasonably level and I was glad despite the hard packed surface and lack of shade. "The level path is pleasing to the laden beast," as Aesop claimed in one of his celebrated fables.

The clear-cut was hideous and mangled. Burned stumps and hunks of decaying, blackened trees, left behind in the haste to harvest the natural bounty of the land, lay strewn about like corpses in the fading light. After checking the map, Steve realized that we would have to travel at least three more kilometres to get to a location that looked level. He was tired too so, despite his grumbling about ugliness amidst beauty, we camped at the edge of the forest a few kilometres from the park boundary, because we were too tired to go further. In the morning, mosquitoes swarmed about and covered our backs like a sickly crawling carpet as we collected our food, hung from a skeletal tree down a short incline. I ate quickly, pacing back and forth to avoid the insects.

"So long, stinking clear-cut," Steve shouted, as we plunged into the cool forest. A few hundred metres down the trail, we passed through a seemingly endless series of sun-dappled sylvan glades with little brooks trickling down through the mossy undergrowth.

Burbling waterfall.

A perfect camping spot, if only we had known to push on a little further the night before. We continued to climb, reaching the park boundary in about thirty minutes, and then saw a beautiful crest of mountains leading down into the Amiskwi Valley. The trail was soft and spongy, easing my stiff and aching legs. Soon we emerged from the forest near a small but noisy waterfall. We found ourselves in a large U-shaped valley curving into the distance. It was rimmed by rocky cliffs extending from near the valley floor and connecting to the above-treeline rocks of the upper mountains. The entire valley, as far as I could see, was burned out. The trees were still standing, silvery bone-grey remains, the ancient husks of the forest. We stopped for a break beneath a contorted, grey giant, with its bony arms stretching out over the path and its weird roots like the tentacles of some fossilized octopus twisting into the earth, strong and permanent though it had not been alive for decades. It was a beautiful scene in its own eerie way.

Normally, the mountainsides look so smooth and green, like a manicured lawn robing their girth, but here the lumpy rocks, eroded and wind-lashed, revealed the ill-shaped bones of the earth—terraced fields with short, sheer rock cliffs separating the plateaus between them. Rock formations and cliffs, not the illusion of gentle forests, were the dominant features. The upper valley was burned in a great natural forest fire in 1970 and the forest has begun a slow recovery. For wildlife such as deer, elk, moose, and particularly grizzly bears, this burn zone is an ideal environment. They feast on the new shoots and roots of plants normally smothered by the impenetrable canopy. As a testament to the bounty of this old burn, at regular intervals along the trail we sidestepped large mounds of grizzly droppings, and left our boot prints alongside the great clawed prints of the bears. One frightening footprint was twenty-five centimetres long with deep claw marks well out in front. The prints of grizzly bears, elk, deer, and other unidentifiable creatures, perhaps wolf or coyote or weasel, lined the trail. I saw no human prints, though. It was hard to avoid the conclusion that we were interlopers in a land where wildlife did the trail maintenance, not humans.

We forded several creeks en route to the bottom of the valley, and about ten kilometres further entered a clear-cut zone and passed by an abandoned logging camp. Tin cans, metal pipes, and chunks of miscellaneous wood with nails lay scattered on an artificially flattened piece of land. Perhaps it was a mill site, the remnants of the final logging operation in Yoho National Park, which closed in 1968. Although natural resource extraction was eliminated as a park objective in the 1930 National Parks Act, existing tree and mineral licences were honoured for years. The tree licence for the Amiskwi Valley was not extinguished until the fire destroyed most of the good timber.

For the next ten kilometres to our chosen campsite, we hiked along the overgrown remains of the old logging road. We forded the Amiskwi River at the dilapidated and collapsing frame of an old logging bridge. Occasionally, we entered stands of the tall, ancient, and majestic forest that separated the clear-cut blocks. Moss grew on the forest floor, creeks trickled by, butterflies flirted about—before we re-emerged into the clear-cut, where the sun beat down upon us, and the earth was dry and covered in scrub bushes. We camped, foot-weary, sore, and sunburned, on a flat patch of earth near the aptly named Fire Creek, after a final push over Burnt Hill. While Steve set up camp, I crouched in the dirt and prepared dinner, our favourite Curry-in-a-Hurry, and we were treated to a multi-hued sunset on the mountain tops and clouds. A waterfall cascaded down a cliff in the distance and I could clearly see north to the end of the valley where that morning we had crossed Amiskwi Pass. It seemed like an impressive distance to have hiked in one day.

When I emerged from our tent in the morning, vast clouds of mosquitoes hovered about me, stinging and biting. It was a miserable and rude introduction to the final day of our trip. While I filtered some water, Steve hurriedly packed up and we fled down the trail, hoping for a more pleasant breakfast spot further on. Steve hadn't had his morning coffee yet, so I knew we wouldn't be going too far. We had about fifteen kilometres to go to get to our truck at the Natural Bridge parking lot. For the first time in days, we discussed when we would likely reach the end. For a week now, I had not looked at a watch or cared about the time—dividing the day into a series of food and rest breaks. Weariness and the simple activities of living were all that mattered.

After what seemed an eternity, I could hear the dull roar of trucks on the Trans-Canada. The forest near the road was untouched by fire or clear-cut, leading Steve to the cynical observation that the strip along the road was kept pristine—"to stop people from complaining that their natural heritage is being plundered." Beyond the pretty strip, the trees had been cleaned out, leaving a barren, hot, and dusty landscape. As we approached the Natural Bridge parking lot where I had left our truck, I was surprised to observe a mother moose and her calf munching contentedly in a marshy field in the shade. They looked up warily until we had passed, and then continued to feed. In the parking lot, we dropped our packs and marvelled at the spinning circus of activity—massive tour buses and dozens of rental cars swarmed in a chaotic frenzy, competing for the best parking spots; people crowded about, jostling to get a view of the Natural Bridge; and conflicting music blared from the windows of cars.

As I stood bewildered near our truck, a hefty couple and their young daughter walked up and asked in a drawl, "Seen any Waaldlife?" I pondered the question for a moment before responding. As the first words spoken to us in seven days, it was hard to know what to say.

We threw our packs into the truck and drove to the full-service Kicking Horse Campground for a much needed shower. We were both silent, locked into our own thoughts of the past week, the glorious scenery all the more wild and magnificent because we now appreciated the effort required to get there—the bushwhacking, the blisters on our feet from dozens of kilometres of hiking on hard-packed old logging roads. All the good and all the bad. This, the first of our summer trails, was a test of my mental and physical strength and stamina. It was a slog all the way through, giving me a greater appreciation for the determination and toughness of the early explorers and travellers. Without our own greater purpose of retracing Thompson's route, I might have turned back. How could David Thompson have pressed on for years, through seemingly unending danger and uncertainty, without a break? Howse Pass, after all, was only the beginning of his troubles.

Chapter Three
VALLEY OF THE MAMMOTHS

As the first tendrils of pink lit the eastern mid-September sky, Thompson and his three men loaded their horses and set off from their makeshift camp along the North Saskatchewan River, in the foothills of the Rocky Mountains. It was October 1810, and they were fleeing a band of Peigan who had been doggedly pursuing them. The previous day, after impatiently waiting several weeks for the arrival of the annual Howse Pass canoe brigade from Rocky Mountain House, Thompson had sent William Henry and a young native guide downstream to search for any sign of them. After riding about twenty-five kilometres, the two scouts spied a formidable Peigan camp along the river, and the North West Company canoes pulled ashore nearby. Although they dared not approach the Peigan, one of them, against Thompson's explicit instructions, fired a shot as a greeting but received no reply. They then galloped back through the woods to where Thompson was waiting and reported the dire news. Knowing they were in tremendous danger, Thompson grew fearful and angered at the foolishness of his scouts alerting the Peigan to their presence. "I directly told them they had acted very foolishly," he later wrote, "and that we should have to start at the dawn of day and ride for our lives for the Peigans would be on us." Thompson knew exactly what the Peigan were up to—he had been expecting a challenge to Howse Pass for several years.

As Thompson and his three men rode toward the Brazeau River, a light early morning snowfall covered the signs of their passing, delaying the Peigan by several hours, and allowing them to escape into the tangled wilds of the front ranges of today's White Goat Wilderness area. But, according to Thompson's sometimes embellished and fanciful *Narrative*, it was the powers of the mystical grizzly bear that truly saved them

A brooding sentinel of Athabasca Pass.

from being captured. The pursuing Peigan came upon three "grizzled" bears, he wrote, that were "smelling the tracks of the horses; on seeing the Indians, as usual, they sat on their rumps and showed their formidable teeth and claws, which made the Indians return in haste." Thompson later wrote that the Peigan "were sure I had placed the bears there to guard the road I had taken, nor could they ever be brought to believe otherwise." While the story might seem preposterous, Thompson and his two companions plunged into the woods and somehow eluded their Peigan pursuers.

During several weeks of rough and uncertain travel, Thompson found his way east to Boggy Hall, a trading outpost downstream from Rocky Mountain House along the North Saskatchewan River, where he regrouped with his voyageurs who had been turned back by the Peigan blockade. He hastily organized an expedition that would bear north toward the Athabasca, the "great River of the Woods," and then west into the heart of the wild mountains, searching for a new pass over the Continental Divide. It was October 29 when they departed the old Boggy Hall compound and wound their way through the foothills just east of today's Jasper National Park. The unwieldy cavalcade of twenty-five men and three women, twenty-four heavily laden horses, and a pack of yowling sled dogs set off north to the "defiles of the Athabasca River," which, according to Thompson, "would place us in safety, but would be attended with great inconvenience, fatigue, suffering, and privation, but there was no alternative."

A few years earlier, Thompson had heard a rumour that some natives and free trappers had crossed into the Columbia Valley by following the Athabasca River, and Thompson had proposed to the partners of the North West Company that he explore the route. At the time, they had refused, deeming the additional expense unnecessary, but now with Howse Pass closed it was the obvious alternative. Not only did Thompson need to get the annual supplies to his trading posts and arrange for the previous year's furs to be hauled out, he had new instructions from the North West Company directors to follow the Columbia River to the Pacific. A rival American fur enterprise, the American Fur Company, had sent a naval expedition around South America with plans to build an outpost at the mouth of the Columbia.

As usual, Thompson was in a hurry, and the overland route north was not easy. Hemmed in by a wall of trees, the track was a narrow, serpentine corridor of green and shadow. Deadfall lay strewn across the uneven, swampy ground like giant matchsticks. The horses became mired in the muskeg, lurching through the turgid pools and shambling over mud-slickened stones and rotting deadfall. Three men went ahead of the pack train hacking, with hefty two foot axes, a route through the congested underbrush of willows and alder. Despite long hours on the road, the cavalcade travelled only ten to fifteen kilometres a day. Weaving a circuitous route through the tangled morass, the horses grew weaker by the day and the men grew despondent and irritable.

By the time they had reached the Pembina River, the troupe was exhausted and provisions were running low. It was nearly impossible to hunt wild game in the dense, scraggly forest, and Thompson, fearing that

Fresh water feeding the turgid pools.

food shortages would erode the already flagging morale of his expedition, sent two men back to Rocky Mountain House to return injured horses and bring additional provisions. Alexander Henry recorded Thompson's predicament after hearing the tale of these returned voyageurs. Henry wrote that Thompson was "cutting his road through a wretched thick Woody Country, over Mountains and gloomy Muskagues and nearly starving with Hunger, Animals being very scarce in that quarter, and his hunter can only find a chance Wood Buffalo, upon which they subsist . . . in fact, their case is pitiful."

On November 29, one month after departing Boggy Hall, Thompson's bedraggled entourage emerged from the gloomy forest onto the banks of the Athabasca River. After exploring the terrain, inspecting the current, and making notes on the travelling capacity for canoes, they crossed the river and began heading west along its frozen bank into the mountains along a "very bad slippery road." The horses frequently slid on the ice, crumpling to the surface with their loads askew. One eventually died from its exertions.

Although following the river ice was far easier than the treacherous forest track, it had its own difficulties. In addition to the bitter cold and relentless wind on the exposed terrain, one night a tremendous wind gusted clouds of sand over the weary party, smothering everything. "The Sand brought by the Wind from the Trees and Flats covered the Snow & was very distressing to us, filling our Eyes & Mouth." The bad conditions were taking their toll and the men were quarrelling with each other, while Thompson was openly disagreeing with his Iroquois guide, Thomas. They agreed on a base camp near Brule Lake and began preparing to cross the Continental Divide. During the next three weeks, they worked hard building storage cabins, stockpiling meat, and constructing new snowshoes and eight large sleds. It was now thirty below and Thompson, more than forty years old, was feeling the bite of the hardships. "I am getting tired of such constant hard journeys," he wrote in his journal. "For the last twenty months I have spent only barely two months under the shelter of a hut, all the rest has been in my tent, and there is little likelihood the next twelve months will be much otherwise." By Christmas, much of the labour had been completed, but the weather remained deadly cold and the men continued to feast upon the meat, drawing down the supplies at an alarming rate. "As usual the men were early up cooking a plentiful breakfast," Thompson complained. "They are stimulated to this by the sight of the snowy mountains before us, and are determined to put themselves in a good condition for fasting, with which the passage of the mountains threaten them."

Thompson and his entourage set off just before the end of the year, and on January 1, 1811, after several "very cold blowy cloudy" days, they were in the heart of the mountains. "The Country from our entrance into the Mountains hereto has been tolerable good for such northerly Mountainous lands." They pushed on past the present-day Jasper townsite, where William Henry remained with a contingent of voyageurs to construct a fort and organize a supply line, leaving Thompson the only leader for twelve voyageurs and native guides. Thompson, noting the diminishing supplies was appalled by the gluttony of his men: "I never saw such an indolent Sett of Men, & in this Time they took care to cook & eat 2 large Kettles of Meat." And, two days later, he continued: "my men did not forget to destroy all the Marrow Bones, as

David Thompson in Athabasca Pass, 1810.
C.W. JEFFREYS

if they were as many Wolves." And, "as usual the Morning spent in eating Meat."

A voyageur named Du Nord was a particular troublemaker. Lazy, improvident, and insubordinate, he constantly complained, constantly stopped for rest breaks, and lingered long in the morning, gorging himself on meat. "He is what we call a 'flash' man," Thompson wrote, "a showy fellow before the women but a coward in heart, and would willingly desert if he had courage to go alone, very glutinous and requiring a full ten pounds of meat each day." Du Nord, with his pestering and complaints, was bringing down the spirits of the others and delaying progress up to the pass.

By January 5, the men with four horses, eight sleds, and twelve dogs, heavily loaded with hundreds of pounds of pemmican, grease, and flour, and seven hundred pounds of trade goods, had passed the confluence of the Maligne and Athabasca Rivers. They ventured south along the Athabasca until they reached the Whirlpool River, which they followed west toward a frightening jumble of soaring rock and ice-encrusted spires around which clung a malevolent billowing mass of dark clouds—"the defiles of the Rocky Mountains by the Athabasca River." The scene was impressive and daunting, frightening the men as they manoeuvred toward the distant mountains through a terribly tangled and scraggly forest. "The woods are always low branchy Pines almost unfit for any Thing, & when on fire throw the live Coals out every moment, so as to burn Holes in every thing we have that will burn." The dogs struggled with the weight, the horses were finally, mercifully, turned loose to fend for themselves, and the men grew ever more frightened.

The valley was deserted and eerily quiet, apart from the crackling explosions of distant avalanches. The brittle, bitter cold and the desolate, wind blown bushes along the Whirlpool made it seem as if it were another, perhaps older, harsher, world. The native legends spoke of massive ancient beasts that dwelt here, far from the abodes of men. "Strange to say," Thompson wrote, "there is a strong belief that the haunt of the mammoth is about this defile. I questioned several; none could positively say they had seen him, but their belief I found firm and not to be shaken. I remarked to them that such an enormous heavy creature must leave . . . indelible marks of his feet and his feeding. This they all acknowledged, and that they had never seen any marks of him, and therefore could show me none. All I could say did not shake their belief in its existence."

The legend of the "the large animal so much spoken of" was reported by other fur traders of the early nineteenth century. Alexander Cox reported hearing of an old Cree who "asserted that his grandfather told him he saw one of those animals in a mountain pass, where he was hunting and that on hearing its roar, which he compared to loud thunder, the sight almost left his eyes, and his heart became as small as an infant's." The frequent talk of this monstrous beast dwelling in the remote valley laid the foundation for a startling discovery two days later. On January 7, "we came on the track of a large animal, the snow about six inches deep on the ice. I measured it," Thompson recorded, "four large toes each four inches in length, to each a short claw; the ball of the foot sunk three inches lower than the toes, the hinder part of the foot did not mark well; the length fourteen inches by eight inches in breadth."

"What can our [musket] balls do against such an animal?" one of the men asked in awe. They presumed the great beast had passed by in a northerly direction about six hours earlier. "I was anxious to see him," Thompson wrote, "but did not think it proper to go alone, and we agreed by tacit consent to let be." The voyageurs and the four native men claimed it was the tracks of a young mammoth, but Thompson suggested to them that it was "a large old grizzled bear." But he knew that the track was "not that of a bear, otherwise than that of a very large old bear, his claws worn away. This the Indians would not allow . . ." Although they pressed on up the Whirlpool River Valley, leaving the huge tracks gratefully behind, the great animal did not quickly depart from their thoughts. "I never appeared to give credence to these reports," Thompson wrote, because they "appeared to arise from that fondness for the marvelous so common to mankind; but the sight of the track of that large beast staggered me, and I often thought of it, yet never could bring myself to believe such an animal existed, but thought it might have been the track of some monster bear."

As they continued the fearful journey westward, a warm zephyr crested the mountains and rushed east, on January 8. A chinook, a current of warm Pacific air that rushes over the mountains causing a dramatic rise in temperature for several days, was upon them. While the struggling adventurers were no doubt relieved and amazed at the sudden and dramatic rise in temperatures, the melting snow was weighty and wet. Their clothing and equipment became heavy and sodden, and the dogs strained to haul their loads, weakened by the friction of dragging their sleds through the soppy snow. "Very bad hauling," Thompson wrote in his journal, "the Sleds I may say stuck to the snow, which is here about 7ft deep." Du Nord grew infuriated with the slow progress and beat his sled dog senseless, flinging it aside along with a broken sled. "As I am constantly ahead," Thompson wrote in irritation, "I cannot prevent his dog flogging and beating."

It was several days of hard slogging through the silent valley before they neared the otherworldly desolation of the height of land. Du Nord, "the coward," continued his indolence and insolence. When Thomas, the Iroquois guide, instructed Thompson to make all the men bring up a load of wood as there would be none at the height of the pass, Du Nord only grudgingly complied, "sitting down at every half mile," complaining and sowing discontent amongst the men. The wood that he carried was so pitifully small that during the evening "in this exposed situation we passed the rest of the long night without fire, and part of my men had strong feelings of personal insecurity."

It was nevertheless exhilarating to Thompson to stand on the crest of land and imagine descending into the Columbia Valley. "The view now before us was an ascent of deep snow," he wrote, "in all appearance to the Height of Land between the Atlantic and Pacific Oceans; it was to me an exhilarating sight, but to my uneducated men a dreadful sight. . . . A heavy gale of wind, much more a mountain storm, would have buried us beneath it, but thank God the weather was fine. . . . Many reflections came on my mind; a new world was in a manner before me, and my object was to be at the Pacific Ocean before August. How were we to find provisions, and how many men would remain with me . . . amidst various thoughts I fell asleep on my bed of snow."

They awoke amidst the enormous glaciers, steep, precipitous cliffs of snow-dusted rock, and stunted wind-lashed and twisted pines and spruce, "cut clean off as with a scythe." The next day they spent hauling goods to the crest of the pass, and camped again in the exposed saddle beneath the mighty mountains. While huddled around the sputtering fire, before it went out from lack of wood, Thompson observed the "brilliancy of the stars." One of the voyageurs, staring up with the rumble of avalanches not too far off, remarked on the closeness of the stars in the night sky in the desolate pass, and quietly said "he thought he could almost touch them with his hand."

The next morning, "Du Nord threw his Load aside, saying he would not haul it any more altho' he has only 80 lbs to 2 good dogs." Thompson ordered him to leave for his insolence and laziness, and relented only after the man apologized, "altho' in my opinion he is a poor spiritless wretch." Thompson sent him off to hunt instead, but even then the man returned after a few hours empty handed, claiming he was hungry. "What," he said, "do you take me for a Horse to go for so long without eating?" Thompson, watching the diminishing food supplies noted that "in the last 36 Hours the Men have eat 56 lbs of Pemmican, more than ¼ of our whole stock; they are a set of the most improvident, thoughtless Men I ever saw." Thompson was anxious to get an early start down the pass before the food ran out.

The weather remained infuriatingly mild, turning the descent into a "laughable vexatious business." Overburdened sled dogs, struggling and panting, pushed their way downhill through the wet, heavy snow. It did not take long for the vegetation to change dramatically. "We had not gone half a mile," Thompson recalled, "before we came to fine tall clean grown pines of eighteen feet girth." The poor dogs slid with the sleds on the steep parts, pulled by the weight of the provisions down into the trees where they became entangled and began nipping at each other until "we had to give them some raps on the head to bring them to their senses." Soon the dogs were so worn out that Thompson ordered their loads made smaller; he reluctantly constructed a cache to store provisions and goods for a second trip before continuing the precipitous descent to the Wood River. The men, particularly Du Nord and his companions, fared little better than the dogs, grudgingly descending at a slow pace through what Thompson called "the scene of wild desolation."

The incline levelled out at the gravel flats of the Wood River, which Thompson originally called Flat Heart Brook, mirroring the spirits of his frightened voyageurs. "The Courage of Part of my men is sinking fast," he wrote. "They see nothing in its proper colour—the soft weather is a thing, it seems they never felt before. The Snow, now reduced to 3 & 3 ½ feet is beyond a thought, yet they talk of 6 & 7 feet Snow at Montreal, but that was in Canada, where there are a great many People." Thompson tried to reason with them by pointing out that it was irrelevant how deep the snow was since they were walking on snowshoes, and that he frequently, even the previous year, traversed snow of much greater depth in Howse Pass. "But," he conceded, "when Men arrive in a strange Country, fear gathers on them from every Object."

By mid-January, they were meandering down the Flat Heart Brook, crossing and recrossing the sluggish and icy cold waterway so frequently that their clothes were stiff and frozen, their joints aching and swollen. The temperature again surged above zero and it began to rain. Fortunately, the hunters were able to shoot several large moose that were stranded in the deep snow and they feasted on roasted moose steaks for several days. The struggling moose, Thompson noted, "attempted no escape as they knew the snow to be too deep." As soon as they had reached the Columbia River (which Thompson still called the Kootenay), Thompson led them south in an ambitious plan to travel three hundred kilometres to the established Kootenae House, where they could wait out the winter in comfort. But Du Nord and his cabal were infuriatingly slow, delaying for hours whenever the sleds had to be manoeuvred around difficult landmarks. On January 23, Thompson returned from a scouting foray and reported that he saw "many large Cedars close beyond a steep Rock, not passable without imminent Danger even to a light Man." Du Nord balked. The frightened voyageur told

Thompson he would go no further, and Thompson, who was "heartily tired of such worthless fellows," was glad to rid himself of them and planned to send them back east over the pass. In his *Narrative*, he wrote that "their hearts failed them."

He did, however, give up his plan to reach Kootenae House and led the entire party back to the junction of the Columbia and Flat Heart Brook. Here, the group split up. It was "a very mild light snowy Morning, fine Day," when the insufferable Du Nord and two others deserted, and Thompson decided to send three others back over the pass with letters to William Henry asking him to bring more goods over in preparation for the spring. Thompson and two voyageurs remained at the camp and began construction of a cabin and storage cache. The departing men had taken at least half the remaining pemmican and Thompson placed his "trust in the Mercy of Kind Providence to preserve us & find us Food." After constructing a rude cedar plank cabin, the three men hunted moose and began work on a large canoe to take them to the Pacific as soon as the ice melted in the spring.

Big trees on the Pacific side of Athabasca Pass.

By mid-February, the men Thompson had sent east returned, bringing additional supplies. The small contingent of about seven men waited out the winter, anxious for the spring thaw so they could launch their boat. Thompson gave his cozy little settlement the prosaic name Boat Encampment. It evolved into the official staging ground for all trans-mountain shipments over Athabasca Pass until the route was abandoned in the 1850s. It was later inundated when the Columbia was flooded by the Mica Dam in 1973, and now only a National Historic Site marker on the shore indicates where it used to lie.

Although Athabasca Pass proved to be a treacherous and dangerous challenge, Thompson was pleased in April when the final boards of his large clinker-built cedar plank canoe were finally sealed. He loaded the boat with men and goods and set out upstream along the Columbia to Kootenae House, where he hoped to pick up some additional voyageurs for his trip to the Pacific Ocean. Against all probability, Thompson had carved a new route across the Rocky Mountains—it was more difficult

Historical marker for the now flooded Boat Encampment.

than Howse Pass, but he had proved Athabasca Pass could be crossed, even in winter, with large quantities of trade goods.

As early as 1807, when Thompson first crossed Howse Pass and built Kootenae House trading fort, he had his mind set on locating the elusive Columbia—a winding river that coils like a lazy serpent through the mountains of British Columbia before rushing south toward the 49th parallel. More than 1900 kilometres long, the Columbia has its headwaters in the mountains of eastern British Columbia and flows about 240 kilometres northwest before making a hairpin turn and descending south through gorges and broad valleys into Washington, then west along the Washington–Oregon state boundary. It is the greatest drainage basin in North America, encompassing 155,000 square kilometres of terrain. The great irony is that the first river that Thompson gazed upon when he descended from Howse Pass was the Columbia, in all its greenish glory, sluggishly winding north up the valley. But he was looking for a south flowing river, and so he had passed it by.

In the spring of 1811, at Boat Encampment, Thompson knew he had found the elusive Columbia and he immediately set out to navigate it to the coast. But Thompson was a fur trader first, and an explorer second. Before rushing to the coast, he attended to his business interests, spending several months delivering the vast complement of trade goods that had been hauled over Athabasca Pass to his trading posts in the Columbia District. It was late June before he was floating down that mighty river to the coast.

Aware of the political ramifications of his expedition, Thompson stopped for an important task across from the point where the Snake River slithers into the main channel of the Columbia, in what is now the United States. He chopped down a large tree, skinned its branches, and pinned a simple message to it: "Know hereby that this country is claimed by Great Britain as part of its territories and that the N.W. Company of Merchants from Canada, finding the Factory for its people inconvenient for them do hereby intend to erect a Factory at this place for the commerce of the country around." It was here that he heard from local band members that some white people had arrived at the Pacific coast.

As he and his eight voyageurs neared the Pacific in mid-July, they were dismayed to see the Stars and Stripes flying from a pole near "four low Log Huts, the far-famed Fort Astoria of the United States." Thompson and his weary entourage were warmly received, nonetheless. Astorian Alexander Ross recorded the arrival: "On the 15th of July, we were rather surprised at the unexpected arrival of a northwest proprietor at Astoria, and still more so at the free and cordial reception given to an opponent. Mr. Thompson, northwest-like, came dashing down the Columbia in a light canoe, manned with eight Iroquois and an interpreter, chiefly men from the vicinity of Montreal." They lingered at the fort for a week as the guest of Duncan McDougal, feasting on salmon, duck, and partridge, before unceremoniously retreating up the Columbia into the mountains.

Thompson was old for a field partner in the fur trade. Perhaps he was tiring of the demanding and uncertain life. He retired from the Columbia District the following year. He, Charlotte, and their family moved to a rural estate in Glengarry County, Ontario, where he lived the semi-retired life of a country gentleman. Continuing his cartographic passion, he worked as chief astronomer and surveyor for the British contingent of the International Boundary Commission, divvying up the land between the St. Lawrence River and the Lake of the Woods. After more than twenty years in the east, watching his children mature and completing his massive map of the great northwest, he lost a good portion of his investments in the depression of 1837. He returned to work, surveying the Muskoka lake district in Ontario, at the age of 67. He and Charlotte spent the remainder of their days in comfortable obscurity, with their daughter and her husband, near Montreal. They died within months of each other in 1857.

In the west, the cruel stretch of land that linked the Columbia River system to the Athabasca River system, unsuitable for horses or humans, became the main transportation corridor through the Rocky Mountains for the next forty years. It was out of reach of the Peigan. Trade and communication across the mountains continued to flourish, and the biannual crossing of Athabasca Pass became a right of passage for new voyageurs. Sir George Simpson later wrote: "it appears extraordinary how any human being should have stumbled on a pass through such a formidable barrier as we are now scaling and which nature seems to have placed here for the purpose of interdicting all communication between the East and West sides of the Continent." And, when the famous Scottish botanist David Douglas headed east over the pass with the annual fur brigade in 1827, he was momentarily stunned by the sight that lay before him as the canoes rounded the big bend of the Columbia River. The scene, Douglas wrote, "impresses on the mind a feeling beyond what I can express. I would say a feeling of horror." Even after the threat

Fur traders ascending Athabasca Pass from Boat Encampment, 1846.

H. J. WARRE

of the Peigan diminished, Howse Pass—a far more suitable and mellow route over the Continental Divide—remained abandoned. Once forts along the rivers at either end of Athabasca Pass were built and manned, there was no going back. Through stubbornness, perseverance, and vision, Thompson had completed the transcontinental trading route that linked eastern Canada to the Pacific; and brought what is now British Columbia into the unfolding political and economic influence of British North America.

In its heyday, Athabasca Pass was very busy. From 1811 to the 1850s, it was the only significant and established travel route linking what is now British Columbia to the rest of what is now Canada. It was the land portion of a complex, river-based, transcontinental trade and communication system that linked Montreal and Hudson Bay to Fort Vancouver along the Columbia River. Essentially, it was a long portage linking two great river systems, the Athabasca and the Columbia. The annual fur brigade departed Fort Vancouver in the spring, paddled up the Columbia River to Boat Encampment, transferred one to two tons of furs into bone crushing ninety pound packs or dog sleds, and hauled the furs along the Wood River, up the pass and down into the Whirlpool Valley. Here, the brigade would be met by a horse party from Jasper that carried the precious freight to waiting boats that travelled east to Hudson Bay or Montreal. The trip, in either direction, took about four or five months. Thousands of people and hundreds of tons of trade goods and furs crossed the continent along this route—and everyone and everything made the unremitting week-long trek over Athabasca Pass. The route was only abandoned in the 1850s, when river travel was replaced by ocean-going ships based at the new Fort Victoria, and when road and railway crews scouted safer routes.

Today the pass is one of the most remote wilderness trails in the Canadian Rockies. It remains in about the same state of development as it was nearly two centuries ago and still requires about a week of unremitting toil to traverse. The nearest road east of the height of land lies fifty kilometres distant in Jasper National Park, but the western side presents even more difficulties. The only road going anywhere near the official trailhead is a logging road accessed by a private ferry across the Columbia River at Kinbasket Lake. Our own difficulties preparing to cross the daunting Athabasca Pass were nothing compared to Thompson's trepidation and danger, but we did have our own logistical challenges, not the least of which was locating an accurate map of the region.

Chapter Four
GHOSTS OF THE TRADE

O n July 12, the day before we planned to set off on our trek, Steve drove a borrowed van and I drove our Tercel north along the Icefields Parkway, past Saskatchewan Crossing and Howse Pass, and beyond the Columbia Icefield. We entered a forbidding and chilly region of windswept boulders and stunted trees, dominated by the dirty, polar blue mass of the Athabasca Glacier. Descending into the Sunwapta and Athabasca River Valley as we headed northwest toward the town of Jasper, I felt like I was shooting into a new land. I came around a bend and it seemed the whole world lay before me—a great rolling carpet of green fading away on the horizon, bounded by the grey rock wall of the Endless Chain Ridge to the east and the Winston Churchill Range to the west. A gold rimmed cloud blocked the sun, yet the land was bathed in the mellow tones of a near north midsummer evening.

Steve left the van in the Whirlpool River trailhead parking lot along Highway 93A, and we both got in the car for the four hour return trip. We could see the gap in the mountain ramparts where we would hopefully be emerging over a week later. The pass seemed quite obvious to us, modern travellers who enjoyed a clear unobstructed view of the valley from the vantage point of the highway.

While the pass might have been obvious from the roadside, it was not so from the various guidebooks and maps we had been using to plan our trip. The previous week we spread four maps of the region northeast of Revelstoke over our living room and kitchen tables. They all, disturbingly, depicted different information. Either there was a trail descending from Athabasca Pass and the Jasper National Park boundary down to the Wood River and eventually to Kinbasket Lake, or there wasn't. Perhaps commercial horse groups used the trail, perhaps not. Perhaps there were logging roads in the region, perhaps not. The trail in Jasper National Park was described in several guidebooks, but the rest was a mystery. Remembering the exhausting bushwhacking descending from Howse Pass, I decided to call the BC Forest Service in Revelstoke. A gruff but friendly voice answered.

"The crews were in there and brushed the trail three or four years ago," he said. "I've known folk who have come down from the Alberta side . . . you can get up there, but it's a real grunt." Strangely, this was reassuring news—at least we weren't the only lunatics following this once busy route. For logistical reasons, we had decided to do the trip from west to east. Because we would have to cross the Columbia River, we wanted to get over that hurdle first, rather than leaving it for the end.

Because Athabasca Pass, particularly on the BC side, promised to be remote and unpredictable, Steve and I had persuaded Steve's brother Mike and our friend Don to join us for a "holiday." Both are experienced in the woods. Mike is the same height as Steve but of slighter build, with an unruly mop of shaggy dark hair, and a bemused thoughtful air about him as if he's chuckling at some personal joke. He is a dedicated bushwhacker, scrambler, and explorer who spends his winters wandering in Asia. His stated life objective is to visit every country on earth, though even he admits that this might be a difficult feat in a single lifetime, without unlimited funds. Don grew up on the Ottawa River, close to the boater's paradise of Algonquin Park. Strong but wiry, he is an amusing chatterbox who takes his Scottish heritage seriously. Why get a new raincoat when duct tape will fix this one just fine? The canoes were his idea. He scoffed when he heard our original plan to hire some fishermen to take us across the Columbia.

"I don't think the voyageurs hired powerboats to cross lakes," he said. "I think we should use a good old Canadian canoe."

And so, on July 13, the four of us packed up in Canmore, and drove west in two vehicles, our car and Don's blue pickup truck, weighted down by two red canoes. In a convoy, we drove west to Revelstoke and then north to the Mica Dam and the Big Bend of the Columbia, prepared to begin our traverse of Athabasca Pass with a short voyage across Kinbasket Lake. North of Revelstoke, the weather, so promising the day before, had degenerated into a pitch-black night long before it should have. Rain thundered down, the windshield wipers desperately sweeping it away, and the hills around us loomed spectral in the flashing blasts of lightning. This did not bode well for the start of a seven day wilderness expedition. It remained dark and rainy when we arrived at a BC Forest Recreation site at the end of a muddy logging road.

We arose around six AM to a cloudy, chilly day with wind rippling the inlet in front of our camp. Low-lying clouds had settled over the mountains, concealing their peaks and making it difficult for us to orient ourselves. The wide expanse of Kinbasket Lake lay just around a point of land, and we knew we had to canoe across it to begin our hike. For me and Steve, the water component of the journey was unsettling because of our lack of experience in a canoe, and Don, ever the pragmatist, refused to reassure us that the canoe wouldn't tip out on the windswept lake. Even with detailed topographical maps, a lot of food, a GPS, and the information that the trail had been flagged a few years ago, I felt considerable uncertainty about this journey. I knew where we were going, roughly, and I spoke the same language as the people we might encounter. I could only imagine the trepidation David Thompson felt coming through here in mid-winter in 1811 without any clear maps or trails. I hoped to avoid some of the debilitating hardships and life-threatening obstacles so eloquently described in his nineteenth century travel accounts.

Don and Mike carried the canoes down to the lake while Steve and I prepared breakfast. The pulpy scum on the surface of the lake was not inspiring. Don yelled up to the rest of us, "How badly do we want water?"

"How badly do you want coffee?" Steve shouted in reply. Mumbling something unintelligible, Don reluctantly hauled up the evil-looking water and proceeded to both filter and boil it before allowing Steve to make a strong morning brew.

Before setting off in the canoes, we hiked the five hundred metres to an historic plaque commemorating the village of Boat Encampment, the place where the voyageurs of the North West Company, and later the Hudson's Bay Company, unloaded the boats after their journey up the Columbia River. A more or less permanent collection of boats and canoes was stored here for westbound travellers who crossed Athabasca Pass en route to the Pacific. The sign indicated that Boat Encampment was now underwater, consumed by Kinbasket Lake, the flooded reservoir created in 1976 by the Mica Dam. The lake, really a great broadening of the Columbia River, stretches 216 kilometres from Valemount in the north to Donald Station in the south, covering 427 square kilometres, and provides most of the water needed to generate power at Revelstoke Dam.

The weather looked grim as we set out in two heavily loaded canoes. Mike and Don formed one pair and Steve and I formed the other. Don, our defacto guide while on the water, looked at the waves, which were now ringing the shore in white foam. "Hmmm," he said, an unusually laconic and serious comment from Don.

"What do you mean, Don?" I yelled across to the other canoe, "don't keep me guessing."

"Oh, don't worry Nicky-Ticky," Don replied, "I'm just looking at your top-heavy husband. Waves and big guys like that don't mix."

How very reassuring. Remarkably, after a brief but frightening squall that kept us close to shore, the rain stopped and the sky cleared while we crossed the lake. Despite Don's concerns, it proved to be a peaceful and easy paddle. The view was grand and wild. Blackened octopoid stumps littered the beach, remnants of the forest before the flooding. The lake was a lonely expanse of water with mist creeping down into the fjords, deserted except for our two canoes. Fog cloaked the surrounding mountains, and made determining our location impossible.

"So, where the hell are we, Don?" said Steve, as we neared the far shore.

"You tell me," he replied. "You're the boss, I'm just the trusty voyageur dreaming of his rum ration."

The shore appeared the same wherever we looked, so we brought the canoes alongside and pulled out our maps and our GPS. Luckily it wasn't raining. We got the

Along the shore of Kinbasket Lake.

gist of where we were, paddled a little further south, and came to shore near Wood Arm, the flooded exodus of the Wood River, which we planned to follow to the base of the trail heading up to the pass.

We stashed the canoes in the underbrush. The four of us hoisted our bone crushing packs and began trudging along a logging road in solemn silence, through periodic squalls. Ten kilometres later, soaked from the rain, we set up our two tents for the night near a rambunctious and flooded stream. We camped in a grove of gloomy and mysterious cedars, which ponderously swayed with the weight of the rain. We got a fire going and stood around it, steaming in the drizzle. After a while, Mike and Don looked at each other and laughed. "Good thing we came on holiday with you, eh?" Mike said, "otherwise we'd be missing all the fun."

A short while later, a small black bear wandered into our camp. It emerged from the brush and shook like a dog to dry its fur, then strolled past one tent toward our 'kitchen' where I was boiling some water for tea. I hadn't heard it because of the noise of the creek. I yelled at the three guys. And, finally, when we all looked over, the bear, as if awakening from a dream, stopped, stared around at our camp—which was probably

Cooking dinner in the drizzle.

situated along its nightly route to the stream for water—froze, and then darted away downhill. We ran to the forest edge to see where it had gone, but it had vanished. All we could find were its footprints in the mud. It amazed me that it had disappeared so quickly. How many other times had I been within a stone's throw of wild animals and been none the wiser?

Later that night, when the sky cleared for a moment, we scrambled up a nearby hill and had a clear view back along Wood Arm to where we had canoed and walked that day. I could see the long line of our journey, one day of our life, laid out behind us, a series of steps from there to here. For the next week, my life would be measured in footsteps. We returned to our camp as the light faded from the mountaintops. Exhausted from our first day on the trail, we crawled into our tents and sleeping bags to sleep.

The next day, we emerged from our tents, packed up in the rain, and continued along the sodden road that ran along the hillside a fair distance above Wood Arm, a long narrow inlet connecting to Kinbasket Lake. Before the flooding, it was called the Wood River and was famous for its steep banks that required voyageurs to continuously ford its freezing waters seeking patches of flat land. I was thinking about those poor voyageurs as I stared down at its surface. Sometimes they waded the freezing stream over twenty times

Looking back along Wood Arm.

a day, up to their waists, dodging chunks of ice, until their joints were aching and swollen. "The water was up to my middle," wrote the artist Paul Kane in November 1845 on his first crossing of the celebrated pass: "[It was] running very rapidly, and filled with drift ice, some pieces of which struck me, and nearly forced me down the stream. I found on coming out of the water my capote and leggings frozen stiff."

Apart from Thompson's first mid-winter escapade, Athabasca Pass was always crossed in the spring or fall. "The reason for these frequent crossings," Kane recorded, "is that the only pass across the mountains is the gorge—formed by the Athabasca at one side, and the Columbia at the other; and the beds of these torrents can only be crossed in the spring before the thaws commence, or in the fall after the severe weather has set in. During the summer the melting of the mountain snow and ice renders the route utterly impracticable." I wondered aloud why they didn't canoe down the river, and Don speculated that canoes would have been impossible because the narrow confines of the valley would have created many rapids. "It's a bit of a myth that the voyageurs shot rapids in their canoes," he said. Before the Columbia was flooded, the Wood River was likely a good waterway to capsize canoes and lose cargo on. "No matter how skilled you are," Don remarked, "you can't steer birch bark—basically bone china—through rapids very easily."

We planned to go at least twenty kilometres that day and, despite the good dirt, road it was a tiring walk. Our map showed the road ending where the Wood River joined the Wood Arm, and from there we wanted to continue west for about ten kilometres on the gravel flats of the river until we reached the exodus of Jeffrey Creek and the trailhead up to the Pass. It was evident that the logging roads were pushing deeper into this area. Many small branch roads spiralled upward into the forest on the mountainside above us, and far up the hillside we could see a yellow machine tearing trees from a great bald spot of brownish, raw, ill-looking earth, a spot that resembled mange on a dog's hide.

The afternoon remained drizzly and overcast. As we trudged along, I was startled to hear a truck approaching. A group of loggers came roaring up in a giant 4 x 4 diesel crew cab truck and ground to a halt in front of us, where we rested against a small cliff near a stream. "You guys headed for the Pass?" the driver, a large, bearded man smoking a cigarette, asked us after turning off the engine. "You sure picked a hell of a week to camp . . . you should have come last week."

"Yeah," we said in unison.

"Is there a trail up to the pass?" I asked, and he confirmed that several years ago someone from the BC Forest Service had cleared and marked a trail. "A guy and his dog came down from Alberta just last year. He had run out of food because it took him so long, but he was still carrying food for his dog. He was pretty beat."

He also mentioned bears. "There's grizzly bears up there, you know." When I told him about the black bear in our camp the night before, he chuckled and said, "Oh no, it's not those small ones you gotta worry about. It's the big ones, and they're up there." I think he was trying to scare us.

We kept our opinions to ourselves regarding the clear-cutting of this historic spot, as well as our previous experience with bears. None of us viewed bears as something to be feared. We always make a lot of noise, hang our food away from our camp, and carry bear pepper spray, and we don't worry too much about being mauled. "We have a greater chance of being in a car accident en route to a hike than we do of being attacked by a grizzly bear," said Steve, repeating his most familiar reassurance. "But bear attacks always make front page news."

After meeting the loggers, I felt somewhat foolish walking for hours down a road that they had just driven down in a few minutes. We all felt even sillier when we came upon their encampment, complete with showers and a kitchen. It temporarily sucked the magic from our trek. I was aware of the hypocrisy of complaining about forestry practices while living in a wood home. The great patches of shaved mountainside, denuded of trees and burned over, were a tangible reminder of just how quickly we are flattening our shrinking wilderness, and how much we are taking from it.

The end of Wood Arm was hideously scarred and covered in rotting detritus strewn across the hillsides. The blackened stumps looked like alien creatures lounging on a beach of large grey stones. Not long ago, majestic stands of cedar covered the whole area. We eventually came upon the bridge spanning the valley, and I was thankful indeed that a bridge existed—even if solely to push logging further up the Wood River. The river was a swollen torrent, brown, fast, and wide, spilling over its banks and eroding the dirt. We rested, crossed safely, and continued along an increasingly rough, or not yet completed, road.

Periodic spurts of rain rolled down from the mountains. The valley curved off to

Black bear shambling through a clearing.

the southwest behind us, bounded by the stony, mist-enshrouded spires. In the rain, I could barely see through the cloud and mist far up the Wood River, where we would veer northwest and steeply uphill along Jeffrey Creek. I spotted another black bear in a small clearing. It ignored us as we walked by, but then, perhaps out of curiosity, began trotting over. We made noise to frighten it away, but it kept on coming. Finally, Mike growled at it and threw some stones, and the bear reluctantly ambled into the bush.

A few kilometres later, our increasingly rooty, rutted road, riveted with the tracks of giant machinery, degenerated into a mangled path through the forest. It finally ended in a vast wall of damp and tangled forest, and a treacherous and slippery cliff leading down to a creek. It was here that we reluctantly decided to camp. In between rain gusts, we set up our tents, collected water for dinner, and gathered wood for a fire. After a delicious dinner of Bueno Bean Stew and home-dried beef jerky, we huddled around the fire hoping the rain would hold off until bedtime. The conversation that night around the smoldering fire, was one of the strangest ever, ranging from Don's dry observation that "pain is just fear leaving the body" to his sardonic speech about the benefits of his desk job. "There's no day at the office," he said with a straight face, "that isn't different from every other day—all distinct, unique, enriching, and fulfilling."

We also listened to Mike's philosophical musings about the humble potato. "Potatoes," he claimed, referring to an article he had read in *Scientific American*, "are genetically much more complex than humans."

"But that makes no sense," Steve countered, "all they do is sit there in the ground."

"Ah! Not true," Mike pounced, jabbing the fire with a stick. "Potatoes exist in a complicated chemical environment, continuously fending off assaults from fungus and viruses. Humans just sit around in their houses watching TV."

The fire burned low and the rain picked up, pattering on the mud, and forming pools around the tents. Before going to bed Mike, as an afterthought, ran from his tent to the 'kitchen' and turned all the bowls and mugs upside down, because "it sucks when your breakfast has mouse crap in it."

We set off on the morning of the third day without a road or a trail, struggling through a world of chest-high deadfall, and tangled and profuse undergrowth. Great spiny stalks of devil's club rose over two metres into the air and sprouted thorny leaves the size of large serving plates. They concealed an uneven forest floor strewn with mouldering logs, and pitfalls into sodden, marshy pools. Fog drooled down the tops of the magnificent cedars. We lumbered through the obstacle course, covered in the muck and detritus, thrashing our way to the shore of the Wood River only to discover that the recent rains had caused great flooding. The flat, gravel beds were submerged and I could see juicy looking wild strawberries ripening in calf-deep water.

We waded in miserable silence through the freezing river, battling the current, and silently calculated that at our rate of travel we would need most of the day to reach the trailhead. Finally, the current defeaeted us. Mike led us inland along an animal trail that traversed an expanse of turgid, putrefied swamp. Giant, floppy-leaved skunk cabbages, stinking and reeking as we crashed through them, were flattened into the sucking mud. We stumbled upon a moose highway, dozens of hoofprints leading us in and out of the water—through billabongs, narrow mires of trapped water, sometimes thigh-deep, lined with sticky clay paste that clung to our boots. We thankfully reached a flat swath of dry land covered in soapberries and spruce. The sun came out briefly, revealing mysterious mist descending from the ice-encrusted glaciers above, and we could see up through the cracks and defiles of the pass. So far, we had travelled a grand total of one kilometre that day. We were exhausted, and it was time for lunch.

The next three kilometres were an easy stroll compared to the first. The ground was a little higher, and the flooding of the river left a wide, spongy moose swamp, and then a pebbly beach. In less than an hour we had come upon Jeffrey Creek, a foaming cascade that somehow had to be crossed. Luckily, about two hundred metres upstream a huge black cottonwood had crashed to earth, spanning the swollen creek. After carefully balancing, tightrope walker style, across the log—one slip would have plunged us, packs and all, into the turbulent froth below—we huddled out of the rain beneath a huge cedar, next to an official aluminum trail sign proclaiming the Athabasca Pass Heritage Trail, 14 KM to the summit. In our haste to get out of the rain, we missed the Forest Service Recreation Site, with its welcoming tent pads on a small island not far from the trailhead sign. In spite of this civilized arrangement, the trailhead and the campsite have no road or path leading to them.

Don and I optimistically put on dry socks, believing we had finally reached a friendly trail. After a brief rest, we plunged into the type of forest that made BC famous. Huge cedars, over one metre in girth, thrust from a loamy forest floor. Every now and then, a giant tree lay flat across the trail, slowly sinking into the earth from which it had sprung centuries before. Occasionally, the cedar gave way to impressive stands of hemlock and Douglas Fir. We were in a sheltered world, weaving our way amongst the towering trees along a ridge paralleling Jeffrey Creek. It was easy to imagine early travellers wandering beneath these very trees. David Thompson wrote that "as we descended the west side the forest trees became of great size. Here we were in forests of cedars of three to six fathoms' girth and tall in proportion, and of pines of seven fathoms' girth, of one hundred and forty feet or more of clean growth, with fine heads. On the east side we were men among the trees; here we were pygmies." It was true. And it

Don crossing on a well placed log over Jeffrey Creek.

At the oddly well-marked but inaccessible trailhead.

also answered one of our questions regarding the legendary troubles of the Athabasca Portage: why were they always crossing and recrossing the Wood River through waist-deep freezing water instead of clearing a trail through the woods? The answer was obvious. How could they have cut trees of this size with portable hand axes, and what would they have done with them once they had fallen? With primitive cutting tools, it would have taken a crew of men many years of labour to clear a road—years to do what might now be done in a season.

As we trudged along, precipitation trickled down from the branches above and the silence was leaden. Soon the trail turned steeply uphill. I was in the rear, struggling under the weight of my rain-soaked pack. Steve graciously took some of the weight and slowed his pace to mine, recognizing that I needed help as the smallest member of our foursome. It seems incredible looking back, but the epic rain and truly horrible hiking and camping conditions seemed to have brought out the best in us. Maybe we were well matched as a group, or maybe we just knew we had to stick together because there was no going back. For whatever reason, there continued to be lots of good cheer. I think we had crossed a threshold and the only thing left to us was to revel in the misery of our situation. It was either laugh or have a breakdown.

"We're back in Club Dread," Mike informed us from above, as he led the way.

The detritus laden track, often overgrown with ferns and more devil's club, took us winding over mud-slickened roots, slippery stumps, and rocks. My hiking poles were of little use in this dense vegetation, although they did prevent me from grabbing thorny devil's club spines for support. Luckily, the trail had indeed been blazed—if not cleared—and an unmistakable series of orange markers led us ever upward. The trouble was, the markers were all placed from the perspective of someone coming downhill. I felt a surge of energy and hope each time Mike and Don shouted "found another one." I felt like a lonely sailor hearing the cry, "land ho."

The weather steadily worsened as we ascended, and soon we were thoroughly soaked from head to boots. From our map we knew we had to head east from Jeffrey Creek to Pacific Creek, and we didn't want to miss the branching of the trail. We were exhausted and couldn't see landmarks to get our bearings. When we got out the GPS to reassure ourselves we were nearing Pacific Creek, the cloud cover prevented it from connecting with the necessary number of satellites. Mike observed with a

Rare open forest along Athabasca Pass trail.

smirk that "even the satellites have forsaken us." By now, we knew we wouldn't make the summit of the pass that day, so we began searching for a reasonably flat and dry spot to hunker down for what promised to be a miserable night. Cold weather, wet clothes, and exhaustion are the three prime ingredients for hypothermia.

After a final steep series of switchbacks, on a surprisingly well-defined trail through large trees, the ground levelled off and became increasingly swampy. The trees shrunk, cedar and magnificent fir gave way to ill-looking spruce, sodden and droopy, ringing the fringe of a series of marshy ponds. The sickly trees, as many dead as living in this eerie region, were slowly drowning in the poorly drained soil. Moose tracks were everywhere, but not along the trail. In truth, now there was no trail, just a series of clearly visible orange blazes leading us through the maze of swamps and over cushy moss that oozed brown water with every step. In the declining light and fog, we could see nothing of the mountains around us—though we knew from our map that, as we neared, the pass would appear beneath the mighty Hooker Icefield.

Trudging through the marsh, Mike was startled by a large, dark shape looming from the mist a short distance ahead. We stopped and squinted as a series of splashes erupted and a huge moose stood up on its gangly legs and stared at us. A calf peered from behind its mother's legs, and they quickly turned and trotted away into the dusk. Our hearts were pounding from the encounter—it could have been a bear—and we set off again, anxiously searching for a spot to spend the night. We finally came upon a small patch of high ground that, sloped as it was, was the best we were likely to find, and quickly set up camp. While Steve and I cleared the ground of stones and sharp sticks, collected and threw some spruce boughs down as an underlayer, and set up the tents, Don and Mike managed to coax a flame out of some twigs by soaking them in paraffin from a candle. Soon, there was a cheery but smoky blaze crackling from the pulpy wood in our small clearing. Ironically, this little makeshift camp in the rain provided us with one of our most comfortable nights.

In the morning, after partially drying our clothes and nearly melting our boots in the fire, we reluctantly packed our gear, and forced our aching bodies into motion. We set off for the pass, which by our best guess was only five kilometres distant. The mist

Lounging at our cozy camp near the summit of Athabasca Pass.

was still thick and concealing, allowing us only the slightest wisp of a view of the ragged grandeur of the wild peaks that spiralled upward on both sides. The mist blocked a backwards glimpse of the precipitous trough we had ascended the previous day. It was a difficult, and frequently wet, climb to the pass, and by the time we could see the infamous Committee's Punch Bowl, the weather had again turned ugly.

It was George Simpson, Governor of the Hudson's Bay Company after its merger with the North West Company in 1821, who, when he crossed the Rockies for the first time in 1824, first noted the peculiar characteristics of the small lakes or ponds at the summit of Athabasca Pass. The trip was an eye-opener for him. Accustomed to the plains and boreal woods of the near north, he was amazed at the glaciers surrounding the height of land "which have bidden defiance to the rays of the Sun since the beginning of time wherever the Snow & Ice has room to collect in the face of the mountains and the valleys or passes underneath exhibiting the ravages of the avalanches which sweep down every tree and shrub also loose rocks that happen to be in their way."

The two lakes at the summit particularly interested him, and he uncharacteristically spent several hours with Dr. John McLoughlin examining and testing the currents flowing from the spring. The two men concluded that the lakes had the unusual characteristic of providing water to both the Athabasca and Columbia systems. "That this basin," Simpson wrote, "should send its Waters to each side of the Continent and give birth to two of the Rivers in North America is no less strange than true. . . . I thought it should be honored by a distinguishing title and it was forthwith named the 'Committee's Punch Bowl,' [in honour of the governors of the Hudson's Bay Company]." On his return journey across the pass in March 1825, at the Committee's Punch Bowl, he began a grand tradition that would persist until the pass was abandoned, and even beyond. According to Alexander Ross, who travelled in Simpson's party, "when a nabob of the fur trade passes by" a toast was ordered. "His Excellency treated us to a bottle of wine," he noted, and they drank it down gratefully. Although Ross expected something stronger, he admitted that they had "neither the time nor convenience to make a bowl of punch; although a glass of it would have been very acceptable." Ever after, a toast was raised "to Their Honours" along the shores of the small lakes at the top of the pass, and we planned to do the same, to placate the restless spirits of this daunting, foreboding place.

The pass was strangely deserted 190 years after its discovery, and apart from a killdeer distracting us from its nest with a broken wing ruse, we neither saw nor heard anything or anyone. The four of us walked quietly along level ground through the summit of the pass listening to the patter of rain and the rustle of wind. I didn't really expect to see other people, but somehow the deserted trail and lakes heightened my feeling of unease. Tendrils of mist crept down from the rocky cliffs that ran the length of the pass, hemming us into a grey and swirling tunnel, deadening sound and limiting vision to our immediate surroundings. The desolate grandeur brought to mind Ross Cox and his tale of passing through "the chaotic mass of rocks, ice, and snow" in the spring of 1816. In the electrified silence after "the frightful crash" of an avalanche he observed that "one of our rough-spun unsophisticated Canadians, after gazing upwards for some time in silent wonder, exclaimed with much vehemence, 'I'll take my oath, my dear friends, that God Almighty never made such a place!'"

When Henry Warre camped at the pass in the spring of 1846, he noted that the "scene was grand but awful in its savage solitude . . . no living thing dared to brave the awful loneliness that surrounded the 'Lake of the Mountains' [the Committee's Punch Bowl]."

Approaching the Committee's Punch Bowl.

For whatever reason, I expected something grand to happen once we reached the fabled Punch Bowl—perhaps the neighing of horses, the clatter of hooves on stones, and the muttered curses of voyageurs leading a brigade up through the shadows. But we walked alone, sharing the remote valley only with the spirits of thousands of voyageurs, travellers, and nabobs of the trade who for decades had passed through this defile. We spoke in whispers and were spooked by the ominous rumble of stones tumbling from some crevasse hidden in the heights of the fog. When Steve tossed a stone into the Punch Bowl, it sank with a muted echo, leaving hardly a ripple.

"Good weather for ghost stories," Don mumbled.

"If it stays as cold as this," Mike replied, "we'll all soon be as white as ghosts."

The temperature had plummeted and we could faintly see our breath. With wet clothes and pack, I began to shiver. The thought of camping here in the increasing cold, at an elevation of 1,750 metres beneath the grim and brooding 3,000 metre mountains that guarded the pass, seemed foolish and disquieting. Without much discussion, barely a nod and a grunt between us, I had pulled out the map and pointed to a Parks Canada campsite eight kilometres away, down the eastern side of the pass and into Alberta. We set off in silent agreement as the rain began again. I could tell Steve was disappointed, but he never mentioned the flask of spirits buried deep in his pack. We had planned to broach the flask of sixteen-year-old Lagavulin single malt at the Punch Bowl, and honour the ghosts of the trade with the traditional toast, but it seemed inappropriate, and perhaps dangerous, given the inclement weather. We could all feel a storm brewing.

I stopped and looked back at Steve, who was supposed to be behind me, and saw him lingering at the edge of the Punch Bowl. I let him have a minute and then called, "Come on, Steve, we still have a long way to go."

He caught up and the four of us shambled forward, hunched and staring at the ground. The wind had picked up and was now blowing fiercely, humming in the tops of the small spruce and pine that covered this side of the Divide. The rain was freezing cold and lashed into us at a forty-five degree angle. We reached the camp and worked fast to get the tents up, selecting a partially sheltered area beneath a copse of ancient, gnarled evergreens.

Somehow Don and Mike started a fire with the damp twigs and chunks of deadfall nearby, and we gratefully huddled around it, trying to warm ourselves. At last, Steve decided to dole out the scotch and we made our toast. We looked up the valley toward the Punch Bowl as we raised our mugs, but it was completely concealed in cloud—a total whiteout. I crouched closer to the fire. I was quietly thankful we had descended from the pass. The toast, which we had planned as a cheerful affair, devolved into silent introspection as we pondered our own lives and the thousands who had preceded us on this journey—grand historical figures such as David Thompson, Paul Kane, David Douglas, Dr. John McLoughlin, Alexander Ross, and Sir George Simpson, as well as all the Métis, French Canadian and aboriginal voyageurs, the native guides, and their families. The ghosts of the trade were strong in this place, and we talked about them for several hours before the wind and rain began to smother the fire. Before diving into our tents, someone would have to brave the storm to hang our three heavy food bags, lying limp and wet near our fire.

"Let's do rock-paper-scissors," Steve suggested, always his favourite way of assigning unpleasant tasks.

Snow-covered peaks of July.

Four fists came together in the waning glow of the fire. One, two, three . . . and it was over. With four players the possibilities were complex, but this time there was one clear loser. Three rocks pounded Steve's scissors and he set off into the gloom. "I suppose I should be feeling a little guilty right now," said Don, "but I don't."

By morning, the storm had blown over somewhat and we had a clear view of the rugged mountains lining the pass. A jagged knife-edge receding into the gloom, they were covered in snow. The pass itself gave off a chilly aura, and I was again thankful we did not camp there. Although the clouds had lifted, it was still drizzling and Mike and Don were wet from a small leak in their tent, hardly surprising really, after four days of rain. They crowded in with Steve and I, and in the vestibule we boiled up a large dose of coffee, and a huge pot of the last of our favourite Prairie Cherry oatmeal, to combat the foul weather. By the time we had finished eating and packing, stuffing sopping wet tents into freezing bags, it was raining hard again. We pulled on cold, wet boots and turned our backs on the forbidding, strangely snow-dusted peaks of July, and continued down a trail, soppy with muck and bog, along the Whirlpool River. It was about twenty kilometres to our next campsite.

The day remained rainy and cold and was notable only for several chilly and hazardous river fords. The first ford was less than a kilometre from our camp and, though it was glacial cold, we plunged through it, boots and all—our boots were already soaked from five days of rain. The next ford crossed the Whirlpool River itself, and when the expected Parks Canada footbridge failed to appear, we waded through at the horse crossing. The river was mean-looking, rushing against the bottom of my pack in midstream, and rolling the gravel out from under my feet as I slowly inched across. I was shivering by the time I scrambled out on the far bank, and so pushed on quickly hoping the activity would generate some warmth. At some points, the trail skirted the forest edge along the banks of the river, which we now followed, on poor, steep terrain. The regular trail was likely submerged under the overflowing banks, so great was the flooding. The rain lessened, and eventually stopped sometime in the late afternoon, and I enjoyed the final hours of trekking to Middle Forks camp. We started a large fire in the pit and laid out our sleeping bags, boots, socks, and clothes to dry in the fresh glacier-tinged wind blowing down the valley.

A sunset graced the sky just before dark, and I looked back on the mountains that rose from the river flats. Perhaps we would have better weather tomorrow. I had had this same thought every day of our journey, but, no—we had walked through the rain every day so far. The next day, we would have only twenty kilometres to go to reach our borrowed van at the trailhead. Talk that night centred around beer and pizza, in that order, once we could clean up and go into Jasper. It felt so civilized, after nearly a week of difficult trekking and random camping, to be enjoying a dry evening at an official campsite with a food hang and a privy. Comfort is relative. The rain held off for the night, but in the morning I was saddened when the sun remained hidden behind an impenetrable wall of grey cloud. It did, at least, remain dry as we packed up and headed into the woods for the final leg of our journey. It proved to be an easy jaunt, with every river and stream bridged, and the final eight and a half kilometres on an old fire road. We reached the van in the late afternoon, with sun beating down and the clouds drifting apart, and drove slowly to the full-service Whistlers campground near the town of Jasper. The trip seemed to have ended so quickly, and I was somewhat stunned to be suddenly driving past scenery at sixteen times our walking rate.

We pulled into the snaking lineup of vehicles at the entrance to the campground, with conversation revolving around how disappointing it would be if we were placed next to a giant rig with people watching TV inside. We weren't ready for that yet. Steve leaned over to talk to the woman in the kiosk, explaining that we wanted a tent site, but our main purpose was to have showers, having just come off a week-long backpacking trip. She asked where we had been, and he told her Athabasca Pass. "Did you have tea at the pass?" she asked. Steve explained the storm and foul weather, and ruefully told her that we had had our toast at Kane Meadows instead.

"Did you see any ghosts?" she queried, as she handed our camping permit through the window of the kiosk. We were all silent. "I went up there a few years ago and we heard ghosts . . . all sorts of mysterious things happened when we were up there. But," she said, looking back on the long line of vehicles behind us, "I'd better not get started on that."

We stunned our server at Jasper Pizza when we devoured four twelve inch pizzas in one sitting. Afterwards, as we strolled down the main drag, Mike spied an ice cream stand and surprised us all when he said, "You know, this might seem strange, but I could

Funky roots.

actually use an ice cream right about now." Later that night, we began to reflect on our journey and what an accomplishment it had been for us. We had added our own spirits to the spirits of those who had passed before us, the ghosts of Athabasca Pass. It seems surprising that such a difficult and treacherous pass should have been the only route linking two well-developed river transportation systems for nearly fifty years. But, as we would later learn, there really weren't that many alternatives—even the tenacious Sir George Simpson, convinced that a quicker, easier pass existed, had difficulty changing the established logistics and traditions of the fur trade.

Part Two
FOLLOWING SIR GEORGE SIMPSON

Looking east toward Lake Minnewanka.

Chapter Five
TRAIL OF THE LITTLE EMPEROR

I n October 1824, the diminutive and restless new governor of the Hudson's Bay Company, George Simpson, arrived for the first time at Fort George (Astoria) at the mouth of the Columbia River, after a three month cross-continental foray on the canoe brigade routes of the old North West Company. His journey began at Grand Portage, on the shores of Lake Superior. With his entourage of voyageurs, he crossed the prairies, wound his way through the Rockies over the famed and feared Athabasca Pass, navigated foaming canyon streams, clambered up steep, craggy inclines, followed winding mule-path portages over rattlesnake infested, sage brush covered hills, and travelled through the forest to the coast.

Smelling the fresh, salty Pacific air, and seeing the white capped ocean spreading before him, he knew he had finally arrived at the western boundary of his expansive commercial empire—an empire that rolled on from the Red River to the mouth of the Columbia, stretching from the barren beaches of Hudson Bay down to the boundary of Spanish California. Simpson was the new head of a fur conglomerate that was the largest business enterprise in North America and the only official non-native government in most of western Canada and the states of Montana, Idaho, Washington, and Oregon. After nine years of deadly, literally cutthroat competition that drove both companies to the brink of bankruptcy, the Hudson's Bay Company had amalgamated with the North West Company in 1821. The new monopoly, which retained the name Hudson's Bay Company, was a complex intermingling of style and structure inherited from both parent enterprises—the rigid, central control and financial backing of the Hudson's Bay Company where all people were employees, and the flamboyant profit-driven partnerships of the Nor'Westers. Old Oregon, the land west of the Continental Divide, was divided by the Company into the southern Columbia Department and the northern New Caledonia Department. It was the greatest beaver preserve remaining on the continent, an unplundered source of profit to bolster the stagnant fortunes of the British fur monopoly, and a tempting lure for independent American trappers slowly pushing west over the Great Divide.

Although theoretically jointly occupied by the United States and Britain after the Convention of 1818, in practical terms Old Oregon remained the sole preserve of the Hudson's Bay Company. There was no competition west of the Rocky Mountains. The vast territory, like the Company's other domain east of the Continental Divide, was comprised of a series of rude palisade forts loosely linked by canoe routes along the principal waterways, and where chaotic topography made canoe travel impractical or impossible, a series of seasonal mule paths. Tens of thousands of indigenous inhabitants, belonging to dozens of different tribes and speaking different languages, continued to live their traditional lifestyles while coming to the forts to trade. American free trappers had begun to penetrate the Snake River country in the mid-1820s, and other American settlers were congregating in the Willamette Valley south of the Hudson's Bay Company's main southern headquarters at Fort Vancouver, along the lower reaches of the Columbia River.

Kootenay tipi made from grass mats circa 1860 similar to those seen by Simpson and his entourage.
CORPORATION OF LAND SURVEYORS OF THE PROVINCE OF BRITISH COLUMBIA

George Simpson made several cross-continental trips to inspect the far-flung departments of his monopoly, after his first trip in 1824. Crossing Athabasca Pass several times in the 1820s and 1830s, he was anxious to find a shorter and less arduous route that was also less expensive and more efficient. Simpson was known as the Little Emperor for his less than inclusive leadership style. An energetic and ruthlessly efficient Scot, who had risen from the lower rungs of society to become the undisputed authority in northwestern North America, he was always searching for new ways to pinch a penny—either by paying his employees less, making them work harder and longer, or by improving on the tangled and complicated logistics of cross-continental canoe travel.

In 1841, Simpson planned a world-girdling trip that would take him west from Montreal, inspecting all his vast domain, across the Pacific and Asia to England, and back to Montreal. He was searching for ways to increase the profit of a company at the apex of its growth and expansion. With no unplundered beaver country left, he had to find ways to improve the efficiency of communication and transportation in the regions already under his control. He had earned a reputation for ruthlessness, heartlessness and stinginess with the voyageurs and traders in the Canadian west, but was a respected and honoured member of the elite in Montreal and London for these same reasons. The greatest logistical weakness of the company's western operations was the tenuous, dangerous, and seasonally blocked Athabasca Pass, the only link between the western and eastern sides of the continent.

Unfortunately, we'll never know Simpson's thoughts on this monumental journey, since the resulting book *Narrative of a Journey Round the World in 1841 and 1842*, published in 1847, was ghostwritten by an unknown Englishman. When crossing the prairies between Fort Garry and Edmonton House in June 1841, Simpson was informed by the "Columbia Guides" that Athabasca Pass would be in full flood, and unnavigable without extreme danger or a long delay, until the water level subsided in the fall. At the age of fifty-one, the Little Emperor had lost his appetite for extreme danger, but a delay was out of the question to the man who always set out to break speed records when he travelled. Long suspecting that a better route might exist south of Athabasca Pass, and secretly doubting the claims of his voyageurs and native guides, Simpson leapt at the opportunity to discover a new and better pass himself. Not only would a better pass save the Company money, but Simpson would be forever credited with its discovery.

He was also concerned about American immigration into what he considered his fur preserve. In the same year, Simpson had instructed James Sinclair to lead a band of Métis settlers, one hundred and twenty one people, including pregnant women, children and the elderly, across the Rockies by Athabasca Pass to settle around Fort Vancouver and strengthen British territorial claims to the region. American settlers had begun to carve out farms from the forests along the Willamette River. Simpson's instructions to Sinclair and the cavalcade of Métis emigrants, however, called for them to cross Athabasca Pass in the fall after the flooding of the Wood River had subsided, not to follow him on his quest for a new pass in the south.

At Fort Edmonton, Simpson engaged the services of an experienced guide he called Peechee, a "half-breed Chief of the mountain Crees," for a journey over the mountains further south along the latitude of the headwaters of the Columbia River. This strong head chief—known as Pesew in Cree, and Louis Piché in French—guided fur traders and visitors into the Rockies and as far south as the Missouri River from the 1820s until his death in 1845.

By early August 1841, the cavalcade including Simpson, Pesew, and twenty others with forty-five horses trotted south across the dusty plains and scraggly forests of the foothills, with mosquitoes "annoying us to an almost insupportable degree." Soon the mountains, "white peaks, looking like clouds on the verge of the horizon," were directly west, and they steered toward the Ghost River and Devil's Gap, an eerie, rocky hole in the mountains that leads to the eastern end of Lake Minnewanka in today's Banff National Park. It was the standard Cree route into the Bow Valley and the mountains in those days.

Simpson's company "emerged from the woods in a long open valley terminating in a high ridge. . . . As far as the eye could reach, mountain rose above mountain while at our feet lay a valley surrounded by an amphitheater of cold, bare, rugged peaks." The troops descended to the windswept sand dunes between the Ghost River and the three round Ghost Lakes, the scene of many fierce battles between the Kootenay and their traditional enemies, the Peigan, who had driven them from the plains a half century earlier. The region along the river was a great burial ground, and even today ghosts are rumoured to patrol the zone, inspecting grave sites, and claiming the skulls of their foes. "In these crags," Simpson wrote, "which were almost perpendicular, neither could tree plant its roots nor goat find a resting place; the 'Demon of the Mountains' alone could fix his dwelling there." Simpson and his entourage camped along the stony valley bottom and then headed through the ragged portal of the Devil's Gap. Simpson proudly noted that he was probably the first white man through this route, although this is likely his own vain speculation since Hudson's Bay Company and Nor'Wester underlings travelled extensively with their aboriginal families, and who knows where they went.

The cavalcade slowly edged its way through the dense, windblown pines and spruce and skirted the shore of the three lakes in the Ghost chain. The final one they graciously "named after Peechee, as being our guide's usual home." Here, they expected

The Little Emperor on a tour of inspection, from a 1923 Hudson's Bay Company calendar.

to meet Peechee's wife and children, "but Madam Peechee and the children had left their encampment, probably on account of a scarcity of game." Here, Simpson was amazed at the vagaries of life in the wilderness, though one wonders how he could have been, after nearly three decades in the fur trade. "What an idea," he wrote "of the loneliness and precariousness of savage life does this single glimpse of the biography of the Peechees suggest!" This observation says little about the life of Pesew's family and more about Simpson and his ghostwriter in London, as the passage reflects the condescending moral attitudes of Victorian England that were increasingly encroaching upon the social customs of the fur trade in the Canadian Far West.

The next day, according to the impatient Little Emperor's custom, they marched and rode before breakfast for three hours "over broken rocks and through thick forests" only to find that they were missing six horses. Imperiously, Simpson "instantly dispatched" all the men but two to track down the wayward beasts, while he waited along the desolate shores of Lake Minnewanka. The famished men, before departing on their dreary task to round up the supply horses, concocted "a kind of burgoo" by "stewing two partridges and making a little pemmican." The sun was out, the waters sparkled and shimmered, and the "perpendicular walls of granite . . . [rose to] adamantine heights above." But "as ill luck would have it, one of the missing horses carried our best provisions." The day drew on and at evening the men had not returned with the horses. Simpson wanted his dinner. Fortunately, "the beauty of the scenery formed some compensation for this loss of time." As his servant began to stew up the last of the burgoo for supper, Simpson wistfully noted that "among the dizzy altitudes of their battlemented summits the goats and sheep bounded in playful security." Fresh meat was not to be had for his repast this evening.

It was here, while lounging at sunset along the forested shore of the lake, that Simpson heard a tale from one of his native guides. According to the story recorded by Simpson, a young Cree couple had been tracked through the Devil's Gap by five hostile men of another tribe, possibly Peigan. As the warriors charged toward them, the young man turned to his wife and said that "as they could die but once, they had better make up their minds to submit to their present fate without resistance." Startled by this fatalistic display, she replied that "as they had but one life to lose, they were the more decidedly bound to defend it to the last, even under the most desperate circumstances." She then said, perhaps to inspire her quavering mate, that "as they were young and by no means pitiful, they had an additional motive for preventing their hearts from becoming small."

A woman of action, she grabbed a rifle and "brought the foremost warrior to the earth with a bullet." Her husband, rallying, and overcoming his shame and fear, sunk arrows into two others before they had galloped up. Reining in his horse and leaping from its back, the fourth warrior raised his weapon to "take vengeance on the courageous woman," but stumbled as he approached her. "In the twinkling of an eye" she drove her dagger into his chest and killed him just as the sole remaining warrior fired his rifle, blasting her husband in the arm. Before she could kill him, the surviving enemy horseman realized he was now outnumbered, and galloped away in fear. Presumably the courageous and fortunate couple lived to tell the story, and after claiming the possessions and horses of their dead foes, they were probably quite well off. The episode was, Simpson wrote condescendingly, "an exploit highly characteristic of a savage life."

Simpson's men stumbled into camp at six the next morning after an exhausting quest to bring back the wayward horses who were found grazing in a clearing about twenty-five kilometres behind. Refreshed as he was from an afternoon of napping and storytelling, and a good night's sleep, Simpson ordered an immediate start to the day. The weary pack train wound along the shore of the lake and by mid-afternoon they had passed through "a bold pass in the mountains" that took them below present-day Cascade Mountain to the banks of the Bow River. The mighty, rugged, and imposing bulk of Cascade was identifiable by the stream of water, "a thread of silver," that ran down its east face. "It was said to be known as the Spout, and to serve as a landmark in this wilderness of cliffs." The Spout proved to be a landmark to a region his men probably wished they had never found.

At Simpson's "Bow River Traverse" (probably near the present-day town of Banff), the weary men cut down trees and built a large raft to ferry the horses and supplies across the one hundred and fifty metres wide river, which had "a strong and deep current." All afternoon, the men laboured up to their knees in the glacial waters of the Bow while the Little Emperor amused himself hunting a porcupine for his meal, observing in frustration the goats and sheep "clambering and leaping on the peaks" out of range of his rifle. "The flesh of the latter is reckoned a great delicacy," he wrote, "but that of the former is not much esteemed." Weary from his sport, Sir George then bathed in the cool waters, casually noting that the "men, poor fellows, had had quite enough of the luxury, in the swimming way" during their afternoon's rafting adventure.

At sunrise the next day, they began "to ascend the mountains in right earnest" on horseback up Healy Creek, but after several hours they were forced to dismount when the trail became too steep and congested. After a total of seven hours, they had slogged to the height of land, "the hinge, as it were, between the eastern and western waters." The place is now officially known as Simpson Pass. It was finally time, according to Sir George, for breakfast. At a pleasant meadow "surrounded by peaks and crags, on whose summits lay perpetual snow," they filled their kettles for "this our lonely meal at once from the crystal sources of the Columbia and the Saskatchewan, while these feeders of two opposite oceans, murmuring over their beds of mossy stones as if to bid each other a long farewell." It should come as no surprise that the governor was impressed with "the sublimity of the scene," despite the fact that it "was inferior in grandeur to that of the Athabasca Portage."

As he gazed about, Sir George spied "an unexpected reminiscence of my own native hills . . . the heather of the Highlands of Scotland." He was pleasantly astonished at the discovery, for, as he observed "in all my wanderings of more than twenty years, I had never found anything of the kind in North America." He carried away two specimens of the plant that differed slightly from the species of his native land. The breakfast and the unexpected reminder of his homeland were so pleasing to Sir George that he got out a knife and carved his initials in a steady hand, "GS JR 1841," into the trunk of an old tree, before pressing on downstream into what is now British Columbia's Mount Assiniboine Provincial Park. The log was discovered in 1904 by Banff guide Jim Brewster and is now on display at the Banff Park Museum in Banff.

Soon after they left the clearing at Simpson Pass, the terrain became increasingly difficult to navigate. The trail, Simpson wrote, proved to be "extremely rugged and precipitous, and in many cases, we found the whole route lying through thick forests, deep moraines, and over stupendous rocks." The horses stumbled down steep inclines, pushed through tangled alders and willows that grew along the shores of the river, and slogged through soft marshy zones before intersecting with what is now called the Simpson River, wandering west. The windfall lay scattered over the forest floor, entangling in the horses' feet as they leaped and high-stepped along the shore of the river. It was slow going, and Sir George was annoyed when they travelled only thirty kilometres the first day. To make matters worse, they endured swarms of a "troublesome and venomous species of winged insects, which in size and appearance, might have been taken for a cross between the bull-dog and the house-fly."

Eager to get out of the chaotic and oppressive forest, Sir George ordered an early start the next day that must have been astonishing even to men who had travelled with him for months. He arose at midnight. In the tangled and dense forest, the guides needed several hours to round up the wandering horses, who had to be turned loose each night so they could forage for food. The party was on the trail at the shamefully late hour of five AM (Sir George fails to mention whether the already weary travellers were given breakfast or had to struggle on for several hours first to placate the impatience of their leader). He did grudgingly admit the skill and devotion of his men in capturing the wayward horses. "The mere fact that the animals could be caught at all amid the thick forests in the dark spoke volumes for the patience, steadiness, the carefulness and sagacity, the skill and tact," of the Métis attendants. "Perhaps all the grooms in an English county could not have done this morning's work."

Modern trail where Simpson lost his horses.

The troupe slowly emerged from the "bad roads" along the river into the Vermilion River valley. The weary travellers had a much easier time following the valley south to present-day Radium Hot Springs along a route similar to that of Highway 93 in today's Kootenay National Park. As they ascended the steep incline to the pass that would take them into the Columbia River Valley, Simpson was again impressed with the magnificence and diversity of the terrain. He was also, however, beginning to realize the unsuitability of his new route as a viable southern alternative to Athabasca Pass. As he passed through a precipitous canyon known as the Red Rock, near the modern-day Radium Hot Springs development, he allowed his discerning eye to evaluate it. "The narrow ravine was literally darkened by almost perpendicular walls of a thousand or fifteen hundred feet in height . . . and to render the chasm still more gloomy, the opposite crags threw forward each its own forest of somber pines into the intervening spaces. . . . The rays of the sun could barely find their way to the depths of this dreary vale . . . and the hoarse murmur of the angry stream, as it bounded to escape from the dismal jaws of its prison, only served to make the place appear more lonely and desolate. We were glad to emerge from this horrid gorge."

Sir George and his entourage then continued south and west to Fort Colville in the present-day state of Washington. Following an inspection of the fur trade outposts and forts of the Columbia district, the Little Emperor headed across the Pacific Ocean continuing on his world tour. It was his last expedition to the Rockies. No doubt he had realized the difficulty of the route he had taken, for no fur traders ever used the route as a conduit to cross the mountains. The logistics were not a sufficient improvement over Athabasca Pass to warrant the construction of new forts and the alteration of established travel habits.

Simpson's "horrid gorge" was later named after James Sinclair and the band of emigrants Simpson had left back on the prairie in June. At Fort Edmonton, Sinclair had decided to disregard his instructions to use Athabasca Pass and opted instead to follow Sir George over the southern mountains. He hired Maskipitonew, a celebrated Cree guide and a nephew of Pesew, who would later become the recognized peace negotiator, known to English speakers as Maskepetoon. The Cree guide led Sinclair's party south and west in Simpson's footsteps. They were resting along the shores of Lake Minnewanka only weeks after Simpson's visit. They, too, crossed the Bow River, probably closer to the present-day town of Canmore, and ascended into the Spray River valley through Whiteman's Gap. Maskipitonew led the entire party along the Spray and over the Continental Divide at what is now known as White Man Pass. The group then followed the Cross River to the Kootenay River and travelled on to Fort Colville. Many of them settled in the vicinity of Fort Vancouver and eventually became American citizens. When Sir George heard of the Métis journey, he compared Sinclair's lack of difficulty with his own trouble and concluded that White Man Pass would be a far more suitable route for the fur trade than the one he had taken.

However, by the late 1840s the fur trade was in decline. With the Oregon Boundary Treaty of 1846, much of the Hudson's Bay Company's territory west of the Rockies was ceded to the United States, a region we now know as forming part of the states of Montana, Idaho, Washington, and Oregon. Without access to these prime fur regions, the company focused more on its northern operations, and the Columbia River dwindled in importance as an artery of trade and travel. The best fur areas had been plundered, and scarcity made furs more expensive to acquire. Around the same time, a shift in European fashion reduced the need for the furs that were used to make felt. Economic and social changes in the 1850s and 1860s were hard on the Hudson's Bay Company and the fur trade. Not only were Simpson's Pass and White Man Pass never used, but the fabled Athabasca Pass was eventually abandoned for continental transportation. Ocean-going ships, using Fort Victoria on the southern tip of Vancouver Island as their base, gradually replaced the overland brigades of voyageurs.

Soon many of the old historic trade routes were abandoned. Without the fur trade, there was no need to haul tons of goods over the mountains, nor was there a need for an established route for large numbers of people. As the years passed, those newcomers eager to cross the Rocky Mountains were more inclined to travel in style than in hardship, preferring predictable amusement to dangerous adventure. They would need a railway.

Sir George Simpson, the inveterate traveller of the Canadian west, and de facto ruler of northwestern North America for a generation continued to run the fur trade monopoly from Montreal until his death in September 1860. More than a century and a half after the final expedition in search of a commercial pass for the fur trade in 1841, we pored over maps and books about the famous journey, imagining that we might follow the footsteps of the Little Emperor through the Devil's Gap.

Chapter Six
THE DEVIL'S GAP

fter recovering from our traverse of Athabasca Pass—just over a week of eating fresh food and taking it easy—we turned our attention to Sir George Simpson and his ill-fated journey to discover a new route through the Rockies. Recreating this route today was not as straightforward as our hikes through Howse Pass and Athabasca Pass, because the topography has changed significantly. Lake Minnewanka was flooded in 1942 to create a hydroelectric reservoir; the Trans-Canada Highway follows Simpson's route along the north bank of the Bow River; and the road to Sunshine ski area lies in the direction of Simpson Pass.

Although a good trail begins from the Sunshine parking lot and ascends along Healy Creek through forest and meadow up to the Pass, no modern trail has been constructed to link Simpson Pass to the Simpson River seven kilometres to the south in Mount Assiniboine Provincial Park. Steve reluctantly admitted that hiking an exact recreation of Simpson's route would be impossible, so we decided to tackle the trip in two segments. First, we would hike through Devil's Gap and along the shores of Lake Minnewanka. Then, after driving past the town of Banff and up the road to Sunshine, we would hike over Simpson Pass and bushwhack down the North Simpson River to the Simpson River and follow it out to Highway 93, which bisects Kootenay National Park. Although it was divided by a stretch of road, the distance to be covered was still close to a hundred kilometres, more with our intended detour to Mount Assiniboine over Ferro Pass.

At the east end of Lake Minnewanka, a landmark ominously named Devil's Head was marked on our map. Adjacent to it was the Devil's Gap, a rugged rocky chasm bounded by a range of muscular peaks to the north and south. The Devil's Gap marks the eastern boundary of Banff National Park. Nearby is the Ghost Wilderness Area, a mixed use provincial recreation area popular with equestrians, mountain bikers, and rock climbers. The area can be reached only by a long and rough dirt side road that branches from the Forestry Trunk Road, a rough provincial forestry road that runs the length of the Alberta foothills. From the parking lot in the Ghost Wilderness Area to the parking lot at the west end of Lake Minnewanka was about thirty kilometres. We had hiked part of the shoreline before, and we knew it did not rank as a trekker's paradise; the path was rooty and rocky, and offered few views of the lake or the surrounding mountains.

"Why don't you mountain bike it," suggested Don, "and avoid the boredom?" This seemed like a great idea, so we decided to trace the Minnewanka part of Sir George's journey on our mountain bikes, and then to drive to Sunshine parking lot and hike the remainder.

We headed east into the foothills to meet Don. He was still enthusiastic to join us on another trip even though the fine weather had suddenly degenerated into something that reminded us of Athabasca Pass. We drove through rolling ranchland, at one time prime bison territory, and turned down a series of increasingly rough roads leading us to the Devil's Gap. A black spire rising above the surrounding mountains was the Devil's Head, or *Manito Ostikwan Wachi* in Cree, and a hole in the rock wall of the front range of the Rockies was clearly the Devil's Gap. By its appearance alone, it looked like it could have been the site of an ancient battleground and graveyard. Overhead, high clouds flew by at unusual speed.

The road led down a steep embankment and then onto the sandy flats of the meagre Ghost River, little more than a stream at this point, then crossed the plain which was the site of the burial ground and battlefield, and continued into the forest on the other side. It ended a few kilometres from the Banff National Park boundary. We parked, unloaded our bikes, and began to ride.

The track toward the Gap was littered with deadfall and blowdown across the trail. We walked our bikes over the worst stretches, passing below sheer, sharp cliffs lining the side of the Gap. The trail skirted the shores of the three small Ghost Lakes before leading to the eastern tip of Lake Minnewanka. In its current flooded form, the lake is a great, long boomerang with its two apexes to the southeast and the southwest. The mountains on the south shore are round and forested, while to the north, directly above the trail, are crumbling rock and cliffs with sparse, though large, pines. We rode over a trail strewn with large and jagged rocks, down steep hills, around tight bends, splashing through several streams.

In Simpson's day, Lake Minnewanka was much smaller, in places little more than a band of water connecting a series of lakes. Although Simpson may have been the first European to travel along the lake, Minnewanka was not a secret. Archaeologists have unearthed evidence of ten thousand year old native encampments near the exodus of the Cascade River at the lake's south end. I was not surprised to learn that Minnewanka means "lake of the water spirit," nor that its unfathomable depths, nearly twenty-five metres shallower and eight kilometres shorter before the flooding, were the reputed abode of a strange being, part fish, part human. Minnewanka was sometimes called Devil's Lake. The damming of the lake submerged the remains of the small coal mining town of Minnewanka Landing, today an attraction for scuba divers.

It took about five hours to ride the perimeter of the lake, the outer edge of the boomerang, although we were partly slowed by the frequent drizzle. Apart from the Ghost Lakes region, little of the spirit of the explorers remained along Minnewanka's shores—partly because it is an artificial basin, and partly because the water level was low enough to expose weathered grey stumps. The lake itself would probably have been better viewed from a boat (it is the only lake within the Rocky Mountain national parks that allows motor boats). Once again soaking wet, I loaded my bike into our truck at the end of the day.

Several days later, we had organized our food, planned our route, and were ready to follow Simpson over his namesake mountain pass. Steve and I loaded our Tercel again and headed west past the Lake Minnewanka turnoff, and past the exits for the town of Banff, before turning up the Sunshine road for the climb to the parking lot. Including a few last minute errands that morning, we had crossed the Bow River four times, all on easy bridges. If I hadn't been thinking about Simpson's journey, I never would have noticed the river, so accustomed was I to crossing it any time without difficulty. To Simpson, as with all the other early mountain travellers, rivers as large as the Bow were a significant barrier. The bridge near Banff carries thousands of cars and buses per day in the summer. Simpson and his party of twenty-five spent a full morning and the greater part of an afternoon searching for a ford, building a raft, and ferrying their supplies across the river.

Just before we reached the parking lot, we saw a herd of huge bighorn sheep. They looked at us warily as we drove slowly by but didn't move off the road and we had to slowly squeeze through. It was a day of mixed cloud and sun, perfect hiking weather. We trudged along in companionable silence, glad to be following a wooded trail again after the hectic preparations for the trip. Setting off on a five day wilderness adventure, with no obligation other than to eat, sleep, and hike approximately twenty kilometres a day, seemed like a sublime rest after the busy time between trips: cleaning our gear, washing clothes, writing up our notes, catching up on obligations and other work, and planning the next trip. It was a pleasant tramp along a loamy trail, with the spicy scent of the evergreens heavy in the humid air. Within an hour, we had covered the five kilometres or so to the alpine meadow at Simpson Pass. It was at the crest of the pass, all those years ago, probably in this same clearing, that Sir George had spied his beloved heather and was inspired to carve his initials into a tree.

We stopped for a rest and a snack while contemplating the next stage of our trek, which involved bushwhacking down the tiny North Simpson River to the Simpson River, a dreadful prospect. Following the North Simpson was likely to be the hardest segment of our journey, and the only portion over which there hung a cloud of uncertainty. It was a funny feeling to deliberately turn away from a well-trodden trail and begin ambling down a valley, knowing our destination was somewhere through the bush.

I had no idea how the next seven kilometres would go. The type of forest makes all the difference. On the Alberta side of the Great Divide, with about half the precipitation as the BC side, the forests tend to be drier and more open, dominated by a near monoculture of lodgepole pine, with occasional patches of spruce. In contrast, the BC forest of mixed evergreens (including cedar, fir, spruce, and various pines) is diversified and luxuriant. It is a wonder to look at and it makes for a magical hike on a good trail, but it becomes overgrown quickly. As we found out in both Howse and Athabasca Passes, the forests in BC can be a frustrating nightmare for cross-country hikers. Unfortunately for us, the bushwhacking segment of our journey again took place on the BC side of the pass.

The first few kilometres from the pass, however, were a pleasant jaunt through open alpine meadow with a glorious abundance of red and yellow flowers. Fool that I was, I hoped it would remain so. The only trees were sparsely placed larches with their pale green needles not yet tinged yellow by early fall frosts. It was only early August, but snow and the first frost can come surprisingly early at high elevations. Simpson Pass

Simpson Pass and the start of the North Simpson River.

was, the highest elevation pass we had traversed so far. The sun was out and we could clearly see the funnel-like valley we would be following down to the Simpson River and further still; bounding the Simpson River on the south side, jutting up from the forested base, was the rocky reddish-tinged massif called Simpson Ridge. The Simpson River meandered beneath its ponderous bulk.

Soon we came upon trickles and winding rivulets of water, soaking from the spongy moss and duff of the meadow and forming into a slight stream heading down into BC. The last stream we had crossed, in the meadow just before the pass, flowed east to Alberta, and theoretically to the Arctic Ocean or Hudson Bay. These first meagre beginnings of the North Simpson River would eventually reach the Pacific. After a short while, we came upon a wooden sign nailed to a large, scraggly spruce tree. It seemed oddly out of place, considering there was no trail, so we crossed the meadow to read it.

"Caution," the sign read. "This valley leads to Kootenay National Park. This is NOT the route to Healy Creek or the Sunshine Parking Lot." It was confirmation that we were heading in the right direction. We continued downhill through the meadow, which began to shrink with the encroaching forest. I knew the easy travel couldn't last, but I'd hoped to get a little further before the true bushwhacking began. Steve deflated my hopes by reminding me that even good old Sir George had difficulty with this part of the trail. The North Simpson River rapidly increased in volume and was now a good sized creek; when it crashed over a ledge, it formed a waterfall we could hear off into the woods. After about two to three kilometres, we were still in partial meadow and we were able to follow the remnants of an old trail that periodically appeared in the grasses or through the forest. It must have seen heavy or frequent use at some time, because it was very clear in sections, but gradually, as we descended, the trail became more scarce until it was entirely gone. The meadow and the larches had been replaced by spruce forest and soon our track degenerated into an annoying and frustrating slog. We veered far uphill and inland from the river to avoid a stretch of rocky cliffs, and found ourselves crawling through willows and clambering over giant, rotting logs and moss-slickened boulders. Time passed very slowly. We became exhausted and annoyed with our progress. Occasionally, we would link up with the remnants of the friendly trail we first encountered in the meadow and we would blaze along quickly for perhaps five hundred metres before it inexplicably vanished again.

Mysterious stump in the undergrowth.

After scrambling along over a series of steep hills smothered in mossy dead-fall, recent blowdown, and scrub, we came upon an ill-kept mound of stones vaguely resembling a cairn. Wiping the sweat from my face, I noticed a large blaze cut from a tree above it. A piece of metal tube with a lid protruded from the cairn, with the writing "Canada Land Survey. Seven years imprisonment before removal. 1962. No. 366," and a symbol of a crown and trees. It seemed very odd to see this in the middle of nowhere, with no trail and no clearing, but it at least explained the sketchy trail we occasionally found ourselves on. We were, according to our GPS, about half way to the valley bottom. Later, I laughed as I listened to the dictaphone and heard Steve's description of the trail: "a stinky, filthy, thrashing mess, with swampy and muddy inlets from the river and infinite mounds of mouldering and slippery deadfall."

We continued to detour far from the river's edge to avoid the periodic steep, rocky cliffs and it was here, along the north face of these detritus-laden outcroppings, that we again encountered the hiker's bane—the dreaded alder. From a single cluster, a dozen or so wrist-thick tentacles, like rigid serpents, emerged into a tangled and impassable zone surrounding the root. Without a central stalk to push aside, it is nearly impossible to get past these evil bushes. The only consolation I could take was that alders flourished at low elevations, so I concluded that we were nearing the valley bottom. By the time we stumbled out onto the junction with the Simpson River trail, it was 8:30 PM. The seven kilometres of bushwhacking, including the first two to three kilometres through the pleasant meadow, took us six hours to complete. Not once did we emerge from beneath the gloomy and dreary forest, and seldom did we cover more than a hundred metres without encountering some obstacle—be it rocks, logs, willow thickets, or marshy areas. I had had it with bushwhacking.

I gratefully dumped my pack on the trail near a bridge spanning the North Simpson River, and we debated our options. It was getting dark, but at this time of year we could still expect reasonably good light until around 10:30 PM. About five hundred metres down the trail in the opposite direction of our next day's travel was a primitive campsite called Scout Camp. However, 6.6 kilometres in the desired direction—west—was the Surprise Creek Shelter, a relatively comfy log cabin where we could sleep without the hassle of setting up our tent and where we could linger over breakfast prepared on a table. These were small luxuries, to be sure, but in the backcountry small luxuries frequently take on much greater significance. At our regular hiking speed, encumbered as we were with camera equipment and five days worth of food, and worn out from grappling with the forest along the North Simpson River, we knew we could easily walk the distance within the remaining light, and then relax in a shelter.

Steve, ever curious, couldn't resist rushing back to inspect Scout Camp to assess it as a potential sleeping spot while I rested. "Clean, but uninspiring," he said, as he jogged

Deadfall on the Simpson River trail.

back up the path, "I vote for pushing on." We overrode the protests of our sore feet and grumbling stomachs and decided to go the extra distance to the shelter.

After a few kilometres, it became apparent that this trail was not a priority for the Mount Assiniboine Provincial Park trail maintenance crews. Small but irritating deadfall clogged the otherwise well-marked path, forcing us to detour around or over it. It was as if a great wind had gusted in from above and dropped a handful of oversized matchsticks across the land. We were, however, grateful not to be bushwhacking, because the whole forest was a tangled web of small grey spruce stalks in varying stages of decay, strewn as far as we could see. No great trees grew in this British Columbia valley. It must have been a nightmare for Simpson, leading horses through this mess, as one misstep could have resulted in a broken leg.

Every now and then, we came upon an open gash in the hillside where a swath of grey, swampy mire drooled down from an embankment and the sickly, ill-looking trees slopped over in the muck. The soil must have been very poor there, perhaps acidic or poorly drained, for the whole land looked unhealthy and ugly. After a while, the trail neared the open shore of the Simpson River, smaller than we had imagined, at this time of year, and easily fordable despite its width. I celebrated our emancipation from the gloomy forest. I silently rejoiced at a glimpse of sunlight, illuminating the top of a nearby hill. My spirits rose from the oppressive gloom of the dark forest.

I soon began to suspect that the map was inaccurate. It indicated that the distance to the shelter was only 6.6 kilometres. When we veered sharply away from the river, my suspicions were confirmed, because the map showed the trail following the shore for the entire distance until the bridge to the Surprise Creek Shelter. It was now getting

Nicky crossing suspension bridge over the Simpson River.

quite dark, and the trail remained in poor condition. I wasn't worried. There were plenty of places we could camp along the trail just by walking off the path a little bit, but the idea of staying in a log cabin drove us on. We were tired, yet not exhausted—probably because we had become accustomed, over the course of the previous trips, to unusual levels of exertion and fatigue. I found it amazing that even though everything was dark I immediately knew if I had stepped off the trail. The hard, packed earth of the trail felt different through my boots. We began yelling "Ay Oh" to warn bears and any other nocturnal creatures that we were coming, so we wouldn't accidentally startle them in the dark.

Finally, I could hear the sound of the river again. We stumbled into a clearing with a suspension bridge dimly illuminated in the starlight. We crossed quickly and wandered over to the cabin, glad to have arrived but a little annoyed that either we took twice our normal hiking time to cover the distance, or the trail had changed since the map was last updated. Approaching the cabin, we were surprised to see a light from within and as we dropped our packs on the porch the door opened and someone peered out.

"Hi," I said. "Sorry about the noise."

We entered the cabin, unpacked our sleeping bags, and hoisted our food bags over a rafter to prevent mice from eating our precious supplies. We decided to go to bed without dinner because, although it was 11:15 PM, for some reason we were no longer hungry. It had taken us almost three hours to cover the distance from Scout Camp— only two kilometres per hour, if the map was to be believed. On a good trail, we usually covered five kilometres per hour, even with our backpacks. As we crawled up onto the top bunks, we relayed our day's adventure and the overall gist of our project to our cabin mates, and their dog, below.

They were Parks Canada archaeologists. By the light of the dim lantern, one looked to be in his fifties, with a salt and pepper beard; the other was a student, perhaps. "Simpson would have been a real bugger to work for," said the older fellow from his bunk below. After reading about Simpson in preparation for this journey, I could only agree. They told us that they were searching through a recent controlled burn site on nearby Hawk Ridge, looking for primitive tools and vision quest sites. With the underbrush cleared away by fire, something interesting might be exposed. Native peoples had been using this region for thousands of years for vision quests, seeking spiritual inspiration alone on the mountaintops.

After a while, we all became silent. Despite my exhaustion and lack of food, I couldn't sleep, and I lay awake pondering the lives of the ancient travellers to this place. We tend to think of our National Parks as inviolate wilderness preserves, but the myth belies the fact that people have been using these areas for thousands of years. These days, massive highways funnel thousands of cars and trucks through the heart of the parks, and luxury hotels that cater to the global rich stand along the shores of every major lake. In the past, the mountain region beckoned people to spiritual sites and offered trade and communication routes.

Over the course of the summer, my convictions had crystallized. The true mountain experience is found away from those luxury hotels and glitzy boutiques. Being "in the mountains" is different than being in your hotel room in the mountains, or in your house in the mountains. To truly experience the mountains in the way that people have for thousands of years, we need to get off the beaten track and immerse ourselves in wildness. It's not about bushwhacking or hardship; it's about being alone, or in a small group, surrounded by land that hasn't been moulded and tamed by human hands, where life is chaotic and unpredictable, and progresses according to its own timeless rhythm.

The next morning, we slept late. When Steve and I finally crawled from the cabin, the two archaeologists were finishing coffee and preparing to head up to inspect their burn site. "You want some coffee?" the younger one asked. Of course we did. I gratefully accepted a cup of strong camp brew. We chatted for a while, washed our faces, and began preparing breakfast—the goofy sounding but delicious Hot and Corny Cereal. The guys pointed out the burned patch on the hillside and the likely locations for the vision quest sites. The realization that perhaps eight thousand years ago people were up on a ridge to the southwest, searching for spiritual meaning as they waited for days without food in this isolated spot, was distinctly humbling. I asked what else they used this region for, and was surprised at the answer. "You know you were mentioning how awful and grown-over the forest was coming down Simpson Pass and along your earlier trips in the summer," the older fellow commented. "Well, one of the theories suggests that the natives went on extensive burning campaigns—clearing out the underbrush, making travel easier, and providing the opportunity for new shoots to grow which might have attracted animals. With all the modern forest fire prevention, and lack of deliberate fires, the forests are becoming more overgrown than they used to be." Maybe a fire would clear out some of the congested detritus that clogged the valley.

Steve and I lingered in the warm sun after the archaeologists left before reluctantly packing and heading up the trail toward Ferro Pass, which would lead us into the core area of Mount Assiniboine. Technically, this was not part of Simpson's route, but Assiniboine is the largest peak in the southern Rockies and we felt we should investigate it since we were so close. Most of our historical trails weren't blessed with spectacular scenery, and we felt we deserved a little holiday. Feeling sluggish from our previous day's odyssey, we slowly pushed our way east and south up the hill through the forest. My muscles protested; I felt creaky and only reluctantly kept going. We crossed

Lingering at Surprise Creek Shelter.

numerous rock slides that had tumbled down from the cliffs of Simpson Ridge. It was interesting to walk just below the same ridge we had seen from afar the day before.

There were few inspiring views, however, and it was not until we had passed Rock Lake that we felt we were somewhere special. With Simpson Ridge on our left, and the impenetrable and lonely desolation of Indian Peak on our right, we stopped beside a small creek for a hot lunch of Prairie Miso Stew and admired the ragged, striated cliffs of multicoloured stone.

As we continued our ascent, the forest grew grander and the spruce and pine gave way to a broad, rolling alpine meadow, dotted with clusters of ancient larch. My fatigue and complaints dropped away—the wild aerial view seemed to suck the lethargy from my bones, and I could notice the spring in Steve's step too. Soon, we could see the tops of snow and ice smothered rocky peaks across a distant valley. We crested Ferro Pass and were treated to a stunning view of Mount Assiniboine, pointy and wind-whipped, and of the imposing ramparts that bounded it. I love the thrill of cresting a major pass and seeing an entirely new valley rolling out before me. It seems as if two distinct worlds live independently from each other; at the pass both can be seen at the same time.

Meadow before Ferro Pass.

After lingering at the pass and absorbing the view, we set off across the back of Simpson Ridge, angling down to the Mitchell Meadows Campground. Our feet were sore by the time we reached the camp, and after setting up our tent we read our novels for awhile in the last glow of sunset before crawling into bed. Earlier in the summer, I had read that sleeping with heads downhill and feet up would greatly reduce the soreness in our feet, so I convinced Steve we should give it a try, since there was no perfectly level ground anyway. In the middle of the night, we both woke up with clogged sinuses, gasping for air. By morning, our feet, admittedly, felt fine, but our heads were swollen and puffy, and we had headaches. I never tried that backpacker's trick again, and wouldn't recommend it to anyone else either, unless your feet are in such a state that amputation would be the only alternative.

The next day was beautiful, warm and sunny, with a few wispy clouds floating far overhead. My head soon cleared from the night's experiment. We ate a good breakfast and, of course, enjoyed some freshly brewed coffee. We decided to leave our camp and go on a leisurely day hike to the meadows facing the mighty peak, taking a fifteen kilometre loop that would bring us to the Assiniboine Lodge for tea, and get us back in time for dinner. Ahh! The luxury of carrying only a day pack! Still, I felt creaky and worn out.

"I never want to go bushwhacking again so long as I live," I groaned.

"Aw, come on," Steve exclaimed, rubbing the scabs and bruises on his legs. "Isn't that what life's all about? I live for bushwhacking." Knowing Steve, no more needed to be said: henceforth, we would be a strictly non-bushwhacking couple.

The hike began perfectly with a jaunt along a forested hillside that looked at Elizabeth Lake, a stunningly beautiful pool of crystal water lined with wildflowers and sparse larch forest. We lounged along the shore, eating fruit bars and watching some people far above as they scaled the jumbled, rocky ridge. Just as we turned around to leave, there, shambling across the meadow, not more than sixty metres away, was a lumbering reddish-brown grizzly bear. It wandered near the small footbridge we had crossed, turned its massive head, and looked up at us with its squinty eyes.

I looked at it. It looked at me. What should I do? The bear decided. It sauntered away down the edge of the stream, pausing only to swipe at an old stump, tearing it from the ground and sending it into the water, perhaps to impress us with a show of strength. Steve and I stood transfixed and amazed at the sight of it. Seeing a grizzly always sends a chill down the spine, afterwards replaced by a feeling of sheer exuberance and delight with life. It is perhaps one of the greatest pleasures of being in the backcountry—the knowledge that we humans are not alone, that the world here has to be shared, as it was by the earliest travellers, with the entire pantheon of animals that make up the web of nature.

What was most amazing was that if I had not stood up at that exact moment—decided to end my break at that precise but reasonless time—the bear would have walked right by us without me being the wiser. Again, I wondered how often over the past month we had been close to bears or other animals without knowing it. In a few moments, the bear disappeared, leaving no footprint. We spent the remainder of the day filled with an underlying buzz of excitement and gratitude that we, as Canadians, still have the distinct privilege of encountering the grand symbol of the wilderness, for the most part a gentle and curious creature, yet still so mercurial and bestial as to be entirely unpredictable, and strong enough to kill us with a well placed swipe of its massive forepaws, or a clamp of its iron jaws.

It is the perceived monstrosity and ferocity of grizzly bears that makes them targets for big game hunters eager for a trophy that they think will reflect their prowess as hunters. It seems to me the most despicable of behaviour to cowardly scout the location of one of these rare and reclusive beasts, get them in the sights of a high-powered rifle, and squeeze off a few shots as the bear drinks by a stream or digs for roots on a hillside. Although population estimates vary, grizzlies can be found only in the most remote mountain regions, an ever shrinking habitat fragmented by roads, commercial development in key mountain valleys, and logging, gas, and mining operations. Perhaps four hundred grizzlies remain in Alberta, and another six thousand in BC.

Yet, inexplicably, the grizzly hunt has not been entirely banned. Money must be a motivating factor. Trophy hunters will reputedly pay thousands of dollars to shoot a grizzly and take it home. Many grizzlies are killed during elk or deer hunting season, ostensibly in self-defence, and more are illegally poached on the ever increasing number of roads carving up the wilderness. Perhaps a grizzly licence should be issued only to those who are willing to stalk one and attack it with a hunting knife as their weapon. Perhaps then we would see a decline in the demand to hunt the remaining grizzlies. If it really came down to a contest between a grizzly and a human—even if the human was armed with a knife—the tables would be frighteningly, and rightly, turned.

We continued up the hill of the Nublet on our way to the Assiniboine Lodge for afternoon tea, knowing the climax of our day, perhaps of this trip, had already passed. The weather was fine, and we lounged in the meadow looking toward the grand peak, at 3,618 metres the highest mountain in the southern Rockies. It spikes upward from the glassy surface of Lake Magog, a forbidding pinnacle of rock and ice that forms a distinctive point, giving it the nickname "the Matterhorn of the Rockies." We admired the view and the surrounding eminences, all massive mounds of mottled rock and windswept ice, impenetrable and deadly barriers that form the boundary between Alberta and BC. No location in the southern Rockies rivals the core area of Assiniboine for sheer, wild splendour and classic, high alpine mountain scenery, and we were glad of our detour to come here.

Tea at the lodge is a treat. The refurbished, historic, log building was originally constructed as a backcountry ski retreat in the 1930s. Cakes are prepared from scratch, the tea is hot, and the lemonade seems out of place—perhaps ten thousand kilometres and over two thousand metres higher in elevation than where lemons actually grow. About twenty people fill the dining room, a quaint log hall with old skis, historic photographs, maps, and promotional posters adorning the walls. Staying at the lodge is quite expensive, and the majority of its patrons fly in by helicopter. The shortest trail to the lodge is more than twenty kilometres. The lodge graciously opens its doors to trekkers between four and five PM, and anyone who has eaten dehydrated food for several days can readily appreciate the draw.

We were the only Canadians, amidst parties from France, the United States, and Japan. Not much English was spoken, so we ate with the others in companionable silence before contentedly wandering back the seven kilometres to our camp. The setting sun bathed the forests, lakes, and snowy mountains in soft orange, and we chose a return route with almost no elevation gain—a perfect conclusion to the day. At camp, we cooked a small dinner and read our books for a while before entering our tent early.

As we packed up the next day I was, to my surprise, still a little creaky from the bushwhacking. So was Steve, thank goodness. He didn't want to walk too fast either. The weather was perfect, with not a cloud in the sky, and it was already warm, rare in the

View to Mount Assiniboine from Ferro Pass.

high mountains, where it often chills considerably overnight and takes hours to heat up each morning. We retraced our route over Ferro Pass, and planned to stay in the luxury of the Surprise Creek Shelter again, to avoid having to set up and take down our tent.

Fortunately, it was a relatively easy day, retreating over the windswept pass into the Simpson River Valley. Travelling mostly downhill, we arrived in the mid-afternoon. It was swelteringly hot, and uncharacteristically humid. Since we were alone, we stripped and splashed into the freezing glacial current of Surprise Creek, washed our clothes and ourselves, and then basked in the sun for several hours until dinner. No one showed up to share the cabin, so we went to bed early when it was too dark to read and passed a quiet, uneventful night.

The weather pattern changed while we slept, and dark heavily-laden clouds crept across the sky in the morning. The security of the cabin encouraged an air of nonchalance we would not have had if we had been sleeping in our tent. Instead of rushing about packing everything up before the deluge soaked the inmost contents of our packs, we continued to sip coffee with our stuff casually strewn about the cabin and porch until torpor and the thought of real food ended our sluggish morning and we set off. We had only ten kilometres to go to reach our truck, parked along Highway 93. The trail was mostly flat, clear of debris, and lead us through an uninspiring spruce forest. It was an uneventful, viewless jaunt to the trailhead. The threatened rain never materialized. We didn't care. On the last day of a trip, all we really wanted was a hot shower and some real food.

The sound of the highway, usually so annoying after several days in the bush, was actually welcoming until we walked out of the forest and saw cars and RVs speeding past each other, ignoring the ninety kilometres per hour speed limit and the signs warning that speed kills wildlife. A few kilometres to the south was a National Parks Monument to Sir George Simpson. As we drove to see it, and to get a clear view of our route along the Simpson River, a frightened coyote wandered back and forth across the road as vehicles raced by. It stopped and looked at us as we climbed out of our truck near the monument, and then trotted into the woods.

The monument itself was a disappointment. Although it was placed to provide a panoramic view of Simpson's historic 1841 route, it failed to mention that he or anyone else ever came down this valley. Printed dutifully in English and French, it was a bland paragraph discussing Simpson's life in Montreal, no doubt "written" by committee. We drove to see Simpson's "horrid gorge" at Sinclair Canyon, and then headed home with a full understanding of why the route was never used after 1841. Not only was it congested with deadfall, but the ascent and descent from Simpson Pass are steep and rocky and narrow. The trail would have been entirely unsuited for a rail route or a road, the prime objective of the next major expedition in the Rockies, led by John Palliser nearly two decades later.

Part Three
FOLLOWING CAPTAIN
JOHN PALLISER

Chapter Seven
AN IRISH SPORTSMAN

"I felt that escape was impossible," wrote the young Irish hunter Captain John Palliser, "so cocking both barrels of my Trulock, I remained kneeling until he approached very near, when I suddenly stood up, upon which the bear, with an indolent roaring grunt, raised himself once more upon his hind-legs, and just at the moment when he was balancing himself previously to springing on me, I fired."

The ancient grizzly, a huge male, had been feasting on a buffalo carcass near the Turtle Mountains in the vicinity of the yet-to-be-marked international boundary along the 49th parallel. Palliser had approached the imaginary boundary midway through a two year hunting expedition in the American west, in 1847 to 1848. This grizzly, one of many he encountered and wrote about, was slain instantly, and Palliser "survey[ed] his proportions with great delight." He skinned it and claimed the claws and teeth, storing the relics of his "trophy" on a pack horse before continuing his journey. By the time he returned to England and Ireland, he had amassed a great collection of skins, bones, teeth, and antlers—the physical souvenirs of his adventure. His intangible souvenirs proved to be much more compelling and significant to the history of western Canada.

Palliser, the eldest son of a wealthy and respectable Irish Protestant family with extensive landholdings in County Tipperary and County Waterford, was born in 1817. At the age of thirty, he began roaming the wild, open plains along the Upper Missouri River, and hunting bison, bears, antelope, and almost every other species he encountered. Upon his return, he spent several years writing his tale in an entertaining and descriptive volume dedicated to "my brother sportsmen of England, Ireland, and Scotland." *Solitary Rambles and Adventures of a Hunter in the Prairies* was a 326 page account of his travels and hunting exploits on the frontier of a land that was still little understood.

On the trail from The Forks.

Although he explored the American west for most of his trip, at some point he turned his gaze north toward the British territory that would become the western Canadian provinces of Manitoba and Saskatchewan. He wondered about the potential fate of these lands, nominally British, but lying in the path of American westward expansion along the Red and the Missouri Rivers. The international border between British and American territory had been settled by treaty in 1818, but it had never been surveyed or properly marked. The land was at that time inhabited primarily by nomadic tribes and, particularly along the foothills of the Rocky Mountains, few others had travelled there to bring back reliable reports. In the years after his return, Palliser reminisced about his days as a young, carefree traveller and hunter in the vast solitude of western North America. He finally turned his mind to the problem of the land's sovereignty—a problem he hoped would afford him the opportunity to revisit the wild western prairie, and perhaps revive his memories of his own waning youth.

The British government, as well as the Canadian colonial government in Upper and Lower Canada, was trying to determine what exactly lay in its domain and how to prevent the Americans from encroaching upon it. The Hudson's Bay Company held a monopoly trading charter for the entire region, and the governments knew the Company was less than trustworthy in its assessment of the land. Voyageurs rarely travelled through the southern regions due to the aridity of the region and the lack of beaver. Their comments on the whole domain were suspect. If agricultural settlers flooded the land, the Company would certainly lose its monopoly, and so Company directors including Sir George Simpson had few positive words to say about the region. One Hudson's Bay Company testimonial on southern British Columbia in the 1860s claimed that the region was "little better than a waste and howling wilderness, wherein half famished beasts of prey waged eternal war with a sparse population of half-starved savages . . . woe betide any unfortunate individual who might be so far diverted from the path of prudence as to endeavour to settle in those parts."

South of the border, hundreds of men employed by the American Pacific Railroad Surveys of 1853 to 1858 had crossed the continent scouting a route for a railroad, and had sent back favourable reports of the farming potential of the western lands. Palliser was well aware of the American exploration and expansion from his own experiences and from his discussions with the Americans he had encountered. American settlements were creeping along the Missouri River and the Red River at a steady pace, penetrating north and west from St. Louis, and north from St. Paul.

So, several years after returning to England and Ireland, Palliser imagined another bold adventure. Perhaps the idea occurred to him while he was retelling startling tales in the parlours of the wealthy of his wilderness jaunt, or as he sat at his desk on dreary afternoons writing his florid and popular book. An inveterate traveller, Palliser was perhaps anxious to remove himself from the stultifying limitations of polite Victorian society. Like many wealthy families of the time, the Pallisers were running short of funds. Maintenance of the ancestral estates and familial obligations left little room for lengthy pleasure excursions across the globe, so Palliser approached the Royal Geographical Society for funding.

Palliser proposed to travel through the southern British territory near the border, the "region along the Southern Frontier of our territories, between the parallels of 40 and 53 north latitude and from 100 to 115 west longitude, which from various causes remains almost unknown." He intended to report on the terrain and its possibility for colonization or development. Persuaded by Palliser's implication that the Americans might claim the interior of the continent north of the border, just as they had claimed Oregon Territory a decade earlier, the Royal Geographical Society elected him a member in 1856 and began to consider his modest scheme.

Roderick Murchison, director of the British Geological Survey and president of the Royal Geographical Society, commented that "the want of information respecting this country is too plainly seen by an inspection of our best maps; which delineate the greater part of the Southern branch of the Saskatchewan, as not fed by a single tributary; while the adjacent Missouri receives a constant succession of feeders at intervals of fifteen or twenty miles." The best maps of the time had been drawn by John Arrowsmith and based on information from the Hudson's Bay Company using earlier information collected by, but not credited to, David Thompson. They showed an unyielding wall of mountains extending from the international border north to Athabasca Pass.

The Royal Geographical Society was definitely interested in reliable information about the southern plains, but, perhaps even more important from a colonial perspective, the geographers wanted to explore the possibility of a pass through the Rocky Mountains suitable for horse travel, a road, or a railway. Murchison revealed a shocking and humiliating bit of trivia in a letter to the Colonial Office. "We have at present," he observed, "to depend on the courtesy of the United States Government for access through their portion of the Continent to Vancouver's Island & the Western British Territories on the Pacific." There was no British road to the Pacific. Athabasca Pass, the treacherous defile that linked the two main river routes in the north that had been used by the Hudson's Bay Company for the previous four decades, was entirely unsuitable. Howse Pass had been abandoned for so long that knowledge of its terrain and whereabouts had evaporated.

The Royal Geographical Society wrote to the Colonial Secretary recommending Palliser's proposed expedition and within a year Palliser had received word of the government's support. His instructions from the Colonial Office were lengthy and specific. After evaluating the potential of a road west from Lake Superior, entirely within British territory, traversing the southern prairies to Fort Garry, he was to explore the Rocky Mountains "to ascertain whether one or more practicable passes exist over the Rocky Mountains within British Territory, and south of that known to exist between Mount Brown and Mount Hooker [Athabasca Pass]." He was also to promote British sovereignty by "regularly recording the physical features of the country through which you will pass, noting its principal elevations, the nature of its soil, its capability for agriculture, the quantity and quality of its timber, and the indications of coal or other minerals." Palliser's expedition would no longer be a solitary ramble across the great plains, with plenty of opportunity for sport hunting, as he had envisioned. It had evolved, under the direction of the Colonial Secretary, into a large-scale scientific endeavour with specific objectives and national publicity, which would hopefully be enough to solidify a British presence before the Americans moved in.

Captain John Palliser and Dr. James Hector
PROVINCIAL ARCHIVES OF BRITISH COLUMBIA

Palliser would lead the scientific expedition, a far more elaborate scheme than he had ever contemplated. He would receive no salary or other remuneration for his services, other than expenses. Initially, he was instructed to explore the western territory for two seasons, later expanded to three. He was told to direct a team of specialists, including: the young Dr. James Hector as naturalist-geologist and medical doctor; Lieutenant Thomas Blakiston as magnetical recorder; the French botanist Eugene Bourgeau as collector; and John Sullivan as astronomical observer. Sir George Simpson, now only a few years from the end of his life, offered the services of voyageurs and guides, as well as credit at all Hudson's Bay Company forts (backed, of course, by the British Government).

Oddly, Palliser's skills, which seemed ill-suited to the leadership of a scientific and colonial reconnaissance mission, given that he had no scientific background, proved to be of great value on the expedition. Although well-read, Palliser was a man of action rather than a pedant or a scholar. He did not acquire a degree from his time at Trinity College, Dublin, but left with something much more valuable to his present situation: a solid foundation in several European languages, and especially French. Fluent French was an indispensable skill when travelling in the Hudson's Bay Company lands. It was the lingua franca of the fur trade—the working language of the voyageurs, and consequently many tribes also spoke it at least a little. In addition, Palliser's prowess as a hunter not only provided much-needed food as the expedition travelled through lands distant from Hudson's Bay Company outposts, but also impressed the indigenous people he encountered.

The only people who truly knew the terrain were the proud inhabitants of the Plains, the buffalo hunting tribes: the Blackfoot, Peigan, Blood, Sarcee, Plains Cree, and Assiniboine. Palliser's "travels among the Indians of North America" and his "knowledge of their habits and his ability to deal with them" were great assets for the expedition's leader.

Preparing for his journey, Palliser collected all available information concerning the western lands. He met with the celebrated Sir George Simpson, who by good chance was in London, but even Simpson could offer no concrete information about the southern plains, and was cryptically vague about his own journey fifteen years before. Almost a decade earlier, in 1848, Palliser had also met James Sinclair, "a very intelligent . . . half-breed gentleman," who had led several groups of settlers over the Rockies during his life, including a trip made over White Man Pass in 1841, the same year Simpson and his entourage ascended Simpson Pass. Unfortunately, Sinclair had been killed soon after leading a second expedition of emigrants to Oregon Territory, through the Kananaskis region, in 1846. On this second journey, he had somehow brought 150 head of cattle safely to Oregon. When Palliser had spoken with Sinclair, the amiable Métis had mentioned his good pass through the Rockies and hoped that it was in British territory, although he had no way of measuring it.

Palliser and his fellow explorers hurriedly departed London in the spring of 1857, and chugged across the choppy Atlantic to New York City. After clearing customs and replacing a broken barometer, they made their way west to the end of Lake Superior by a series of jaunts aboard railroads, stagecoaches, and steamships. Here, a guide, sixteen voyageurs, and two huge canoes awaited their arrival. After heading west through a series of rivers, lakes, and portages, they arrived at Fort Garry along the Red River and then headed south to Pembina Mountain and Turtle Mountain and began their first season's reconnaissance in the prairie. It was an exciting time, as they progressed through a land that was barren and dry with stunted trees and ill-looking shrubs and grasses. Palliser advised against its value as agricultural land. He correctly predicted the devastation of regional drought—a great burden to farmers in the Depression of the 1930s. Modern irrigation and fertilization, however, have allowed much of this region to flourish. The agricultural settlement of this area has always been controversial because of the expense of irrigation relative to production.

When the cold winds came in November, the men retreated to the relative comfort of various Hudson's Bay Company forts as winter bases. Palliser returned east to Detroit, Toronto, and New York to send dispatches off to England requesting funding for another season. After one summer and fall on the prairies, he had begun to realize the vast expanse of the land.

In the spring of 1858, the expedition trundled across the prairie and followed the South Saskatchewan River and the Bow River toward the foothills, west of present-day Calgary. Palliser spied a herd of buffalo in a small patch of prairie with a good view of the mountains, and organized a great hunt to stock up on meat. The great beasts "were in such numbers that their peculiar grunt sounded like the roar of distant rapids in a large river, and causing a vibration also something like a trembling in the ground."

Ascending a ridge, Palliser beheld four or five thousand buffalo "some lying down, some grazing with the old bulls in the outskirts . . . the wolves sneaked out from their secluded nooks here and there and posted themselves in favourable positions to enjoy the scene which they knew well enough would also leave a meal to themselves."

Antelope mingled with the great herd, while squawking ravens flapped overhead. The hunters readied themselves and their horses. As they galloped downhill, the buffalo leaped up and began a "steady lope, crowding gradually into a thick black mass." After a furious chase, the horses outran the old bulls, who "stood blown and staring after they had made ineffectual attempts at charging the hunters," who pursued the speedy cows. The cows made for better eating. Seventeen cows were shot and dragged back to the camp, and Palliser noted that they were "now not only sufficiently provided with meat for our present wants, but also enough to dry and preserve for the expeditions contemplated in the mountains." He called their evening camp Slaughter Camp and, after gorging on the roasted humps, they "enjoyed a magnificent view of the Rocky Mountains as the sun set behind their snowy peaks." For several days, they cut the meat into strips and hung it to dry.

Here they split up. Blackiston, who had previously headed north along the North Saskatchewan to take "magnetical observations," was instructed to follow the prairie south and then west to explore the North and South Kootenay Passes, "a crossing place of the Mountains known only by name to white people," in the Crowsnest–Waterton Lakes region. Hector and Bourgeau set off west along the Bow River into the Rockies. After passing the Healy Creek, the creek Simpson had followed west in 1841, Bourgeau hunkered down to collect plants. Hector, his Stoney guide (whom he called Nimrod because he was unable to pronounce the man's true name), and several voyageurs continued west, crossing Vermilion Pass and descending to the Kootenay River valley, where they turned north, searching for the Columbia River. Animals were sparse in this portion of the mountains and they soon ran short of provisions. For a while, they satisfied their growling bellies with little other than wild berries.

Following a river back east toward the Great Divide, weakened by several days of starvation rations, Hector was kicked in the chest by his horse and crumpled unconscious for several hours. As he roused himself, his concerned men pressed close and insisted he sign a statement outlining his accident—in case he should die they wanted it clear that they had not harmed him or mutinied. Hector named the river the Kicking Horse and followed it east to the Continental Divide and over a pass now known as the Kicking Horse Pass. Today, the railway and the Trans-Canada Highway follow this route. After meeting a band of Assiniboine, or Stoney, on the eastern side of the Divide, feasting on moose meat, and recuperating from his ill-fated journey, Hector turned north. He thrashed his way through the scraggly pine forest along the Bow River over Bow Pass, now the route of the Icefields Parkway, and then tried to push west through the abandoned Howse Pass. He found and named Glacier Lake, but was turned back from the pass because of the congested, tangled undergrowth. All traces of the trade route used fifty years earlier had been consumed by the creeping forest.

Meanwhile, Palliser and Sullivan and several men followed the foothills south to the international boundary for a week before returning and entering the Kananaskis Valley on August 18, 1858. Then they set off south along the Kananaskis River, which Palliser named, in search of the pass Sinclair had told him about a decade earlier. They slogged through a dry forest of lodgepole pine into an increasingly narrow valley. The pack horses clambered over and around treacherous mounds of deadfall, following the Kananaskis River south to a series of lakes. They crossed the Great Divide at one of several possible locations that even today have not been conclusively identified. As Irene Spry commented in the introduction to *The Papers of the Palliser Expedition 1857–1860:* "where exactly the Expedition went in certain sections of its route has given rise to a number of controversies, notably about which pass Palliser used going westward in 1858. . . . The information given in the Journal is, at certain points, too meagre to allow precise identification of the line of travel." Palliser described the route as "arduous" but not "formidable." The "principal difficulty to be overcome," Palliser wrote of his route, "was the amount of timber to be cut in order to allow the horses to force their way through it . . . hard work it was."

His journal clearly describes the forest they slowly wandered through as scraggly and burnt over, with the trees a cindered latticework. The small cavalcade slowly wound its way along the river, and Palliser, revealing his true passion even in the dry, official papers of the expedition, diligently recorded any animals they hunted, including how they were killed. He also recorded numerous grizzly bear sightings, and the sites of their dens, one of which was situated only six metres from the travellers' camp. "Some of these grizzly bears are of an enormous size," he wrote. "They are fond of the turpentine of the pines, and are capable, when standing on their hind legs, of reaching up the stems of the trees, and stripping off their bark to the height of nine or ten feet, in order to obtain the turpentine that oozes out."

After several days of slogging, they neared a "patch of sward," where the "wild and beautiful Kananaskis River leaps over a ledge of rock in its valley from the height of twenty feet, and rushes on its way through a dense forest of pines." The falls no longer exist because of hydro development on the Kananaskis Lakes, but, according to Spry, the site was near the mouth of Pocaterra Creek. Palliser killed two elks. That evening the men lit a large fire, roasted the meat, and debated their options. The camp was just downstream from Lower Kananaskis Lake, and Palliser could see clearly the jagged grey promontories that lined the Great Divide to the west, and the rolling gentle forest-covered hummock that lay to the south.

During the several days that the men "cut up and secured our meat" (from the two elk, presumably), Palliser or Sullivan must have climbed to the summit of the nearby south-leading Elk Pass. Without mentioning the excursion in his journal, Palliser comments that "from a lake at the base of the more southerly mountain a large tributary of the Kootenie has its source; and after an almost due southerly course it joins the main stream near the 49th parallel of north latitude. This river is hemmed in on either side by mountains, the sides of which rise almost perpendicularly from its surface." Although it is not recorded, someone must have followed the valley south to have determined where today's Elk River enters the Kootenay River.

After breaking camp, Palliser led his troupe west to the base of a large mountain and prepared to continue up and over the watershed. They forded the Kananaskis River, and likely followed the west shore of Lower Kananaskis Lake before coming upon "a magnificent lake, hemmed in by mountains, and studded by numerous islets, very thickly wooded." The Upper Kananaskis Lake was a favourite hunting ground of the Kootenay, who for centuries had crossed over either North or South Kananaskis Passes and then hunted the elk that inhabited the region. The elk, Palliser recorded, is "an animal which seems to prefer these wooded islands to the denser forests on the shore." Unable to reach the island-dwelling elk without a boat, they caught and cooked several plump trout from the lake instead.

On August 21, they began skirting the edge of the lake, heading west toward a defile in the grey spires where turbulent dark clouds lurked. Palliser was probably following the scratchy outline of the ancient Kootenay trail. Nearing the scene of a massive landslide, where clunky grey boulders lay strewn along the shore "in a singularly artificial manner," one of their horses "strangely enough, adopted the other alternative of swimming across the lake." Certainly the poor horse was pleased to be delivered from its painstaking predicament, but it caused Palliser "serious misfortune and dismay" as the horse's "pack contained our only luxuries, our tea, our sugar, and our bedding." That night, after salvaging what they could of the sodden goods, they feasted on fire-roasted grouse and owls and camped beneath a "lofty cone-shaped mountain [that] reared its apex to a great height, the passing clouds sometimes hiding its summit from view."

The next day, Sunday, August 22, the pack train wound its way up in elevation. It was an uneventful and not too difficult ascent to the height of land, which they reached

Would you put a railroad through here?

by about two PM. "Our course was circuitous," Palliser noted, "owing to the rocky nature of the summit level, which was not altogether devoid of timber." That night, they set up camp along the grassy shores of a small lake and spied water trickling away to the west. "[T]o the Pacific Ocean," Palliser observed optimistically. Like Simpson, and Thompson before him, and probably following a tradition common to all the fur traders who crossed the Continental Divide, Palliser noted with pleasure that he filled from this west-leading rivulet his "tea kettle, while our scanty supper of tough elk meat was boiling in the waters of the Saskatchewan." The only animal they saw was a marmot, small and shrill, yet "excellent eating when fat." After dinner, misty clouds floated from the west and clung to the mountains above. "This," Palliser ruefully recorded, "combined with our proximity to the glaciers on either side, and the scarcity of wood for our camp fire, caused us to pass a chill and uncomfortable night."

In the morning, they saddled up and "commenced our descent of the western slope of the Rocky Mountains." Leading the horses along the small, west-leading stream, Palliser "observed it grow larger and larger" down a treacherously steep and rocky slope to the floor of a narrow, v-shaped valley. "The men ever afterwards called it Palliser's River," Palliser wrote humbly. As they rode down the Palliser River, they noted the "remarkable change in the increased luxuriance of the vegetation, and also the appearance of shrubs that we had not seen on the eastern side of the mountains." The greatest obstacle to their travel was the thickness of the forest and the quantity of deadfall—the horses sometimes walked down the centre of the river to avoid the tangled mess in the narrow valley. As the valley widened, the river remained broad and shallow, then passed through a chasm before disgorging into the Kootenay River.

They eventually camped near the headwaters of the Columbia, before meeting up with a band of Kootenay on the Tobacco Plains to the south. On September 1, Palliser prepared to recross the Rockies, initially heading for a promising-looking gap in the wall of mountains, but retreated when it became too treacherous to continue. Instead, his group meandered south toward North Kootenay Pass. After bartering for some fresh horses and food from the Kootenay, Palliser led his group across the Elk River, and looked north up the valley toward the Elk Pass access to the Kananaskis Lakes—the same valley that is so accurately described in his journal, but without a narrative of its exploration. After crossing North Kootenay Pass and making his way through the foothills to the prairie, Palliser headed north to Fort Edmonton.

In the winter of 1858 to 1859, the entire party of six and the voyageurs regrouped at Fort Edmonton. A massive palisade structure overlooking the broad North Saskatchewan River, Fort Edmonton was the largest fur trade outpost in the west, and the closest thing to a small town in the entire region. Palliser, after hearing and reading the reports of the various branches of his expedition, confidently wrote a report outlining his optimistic opinions on the Rocky Mountain passes, and was particularly favourable about the prospect of a pass within British territory. "I am rejoiced to say," he wrote, "that I have completely succeeded in discovering not only a pass practicable for horses, but one which, with but little expense, could be rendered available for carts also. This pass will connect the prairies of the Saskatchewan with Her Majesty's possessions on the west side of the Rocky Mountains. The pass is situated precisely where I had long supposed, and this impression was communicated by me to Her Majesty's Government previous to my appointment to the command of the Expedition."

Palliser could have been referring to Vermilion Pass, which allows easy access to the west side of the divide into the upper Kootenay River, but then requires a long detour south to circumvent the rugged range that separates the Kootenay from the Columbia. The thought of driving a car or riding a train over two other passes Palliser may have been referring to, North and South Kananaskis Passes, would shake the foundations of the bravest soul. Elk Pass, on the other hand, leading south from the Kananaskis Lakes, also provides an easy crossing of the divide but has a long southern detour before a traveller could resume westward travel. Elk Pass is the only suitable pass that cattle could have crossed, so Sinclair's route in 1854 was probably over Elk Pass. Unfortunately, while its southern trajectory was no problem for Sinclair and his emigrants en route to Oregon, it would have been of little use for Palliser and his objective of securing a route well north of the international border.

During the winter, and the following summer of 1859, Hector continued his scouting of the Rockies north of the Kananaskis, eventually pushing his way through Howse Pass and down the Blaeberry River. Palliser led the rest of the group south along the edge of the foothills, through the territory of the Peigan, and over North Kootenay Pass, exploring the region to the west of the Rockies, before heading to Fort Colville in Washington. There he met up with Hector before continuing down the Columbia to Fort Vancouver, and sailing for home in 1860. Of the entire group only Hector, who emigrated to New Zealand in the 1860s and became a well-known geologist, ever returned to the Canadian west. In 1905, Hector travelled by train through the Kicking Horse Pass he had pioneered in his youth. Palliser participated in the American Civil War as a British agent, went on several other major hunting expeditions around the globe, and spent the remainder of his days managing the family estate in Ireland. He wrote longingly of returning to "those old wilds," but never made the trip. He died at the age of seventy, in 1887. He had received several awards for his work exploring the Canadian west, including the Gold Patron's Medal from the Royal Geographical Society. Eventually, after the Civil War, when the importance of his expedition became more apparent, the British government gave him the official recognition he deserved.

Soon after Palliser returned to Britain in 1860, he confronted the task of compiling his information into a report that was eventually published, along with maps, in 1863. Although Palliser's map is emblazoned with the warning, "the above is only a rough sketch," it clearly shows the Kananaskis River and the Kananaskis Lakes and a pass directly to the west, marked as "Height of Land." Elk Pass, and the entire Elk Valley, seemingly contradicting Palliser's accurate description in his Journal, remain as blank spaces.

Palliser had many detractors, including high-placed politicians who were also directors of the Hudson's Bay Company angered by his recommendation to end their monopoly. Still, his report clearly but roughly laid out the geography of the southern Rockies and published it for the first time. His measurements of elevation and map points, however crude, were of great benefit to Arrowsmith in updating the rudimentary sketches that had previously counted as maps of the region, providing the first reasonably accurate delineation of the southern Rockies—the basic structure of the mountainous terrain south of Athabasca Pass. Tellingly, Palliser concluded that the greatest difficulty for a railroad or horse trail would lie in the next range of mountains, the Selkirks and Purcells, the misty spires lodged between the big bend of the Columbia. This was the problem most noted by Palliser in the detailed reports that he and Hector and the others prepared after returning to England. Palliser observed that while it would prove relatively feasible to breach the main range of the Rockies, the mountains further west might make such passes as the Kicking Horse, Kananaskis, and Vermilion of limited use.

Palliser was not confident that a cost-effective route could be established entirely within British Territory and south of the big bend of the Columbia. "The knowledge of the country on the whole," he wrote, "would never lead me to advocate a line of communication from Canada across the continent to the Pacific . . . the unfortunate choice of an astronomical boundary line has completely isolated the Central American possessions of Great Britain from Canada in the east, and also almost debarred them from any eligible access from the Pacific coast on the west." He instead suggested a more northerly mountain crossing, and the use of a series of steamships along the Columbia and the lakes of interior British Columbia. Spry wrote that "the fact that the Canadian Pacific Railway was eventually built through the Rockies to the Pacific, does not discredit Palliser's judgment; the difficulties and expense that beset this astonishing feat of railroading certainly suggest that Palliser had not exaggerated the engineering difficulties and economic costs which the young Canada was ultimately to overcome in establishing its boundaries from sea to sea."

The need for a British route connecting the colonies on the Pacific to the interior of the continent grew significantly after gold was discovered on the Fraser River in 1858, the same year that Palliser and Sullivan crossed Kananaskis Pass and Hector scouted Kicking Horse and Vermilion Passes. With the beginning of the American Civil War in 1861, however, the year after Palliser returned to England and presented his findings to the government, American westward expansion stalled temporarily, relieving the pressure for a road to assert British sovereignty over the region. When railway surveyors scouted the land years later, they chose, for a variety of reasons, the Kicking Horse Pass for the railway. The Trans-Canada Highway followed in 1962. Hector's Vermilion Pass became the site of the first road through the Rockies, the Banff–Windermere Highway.

All of the passes followed by Palliser himself in 1858—Elk Pass and the North or South Kananaskis Passes—remain undeveloped. In Alberta, they can be reached from Peter Lougheed Provincial Park, a part of the larger provincial recreation area of Kananaskis Country. Elk Pass descends into British Columbia's Elk Lakes Provincial Park, while the North and South Kananaskis Passes descend into Height of the

Rockies Provincial Park. Hikers who follow Palliser's footsteps today can explore some of the most beautiful terrain in the Canadian Rockies, and many of the distinguishing landforms he described are immediately and strikingly apparent. Although there remains controversy over what pass Palliser actually crossed, and what pass he recommended to the government, for modern adventurers on a historic quest, this was all the excuse we needed to check out all three.

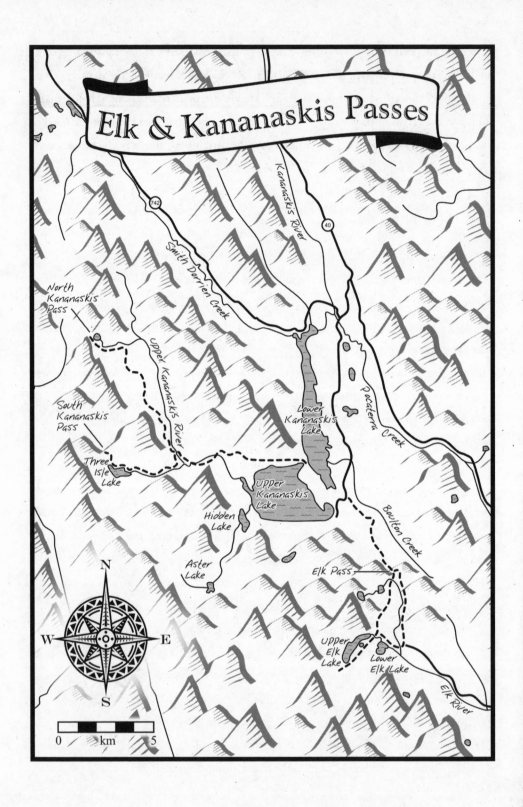

Elk & Kananaskis Passes

742

Kananaskis River

40

Smith Dorrien Creek

North Kananaskis Pass

South Kananaskis Pass

Upper Kananaskis River

Three Isle Lake

Lower Kananaskis Lake

Upper Kananaskis Lake

Pocaterra Creek

Hidden Lake

Boulton Creek

Aster Lake

Elk Pass

Upper Elk Lake

Lower Elk Lake

Elk River

N

W E

S

0 km 5

Chapter Eight
THE MYSTERY OF KANANASKIS

J ohn Palliser's name appears all over the maps of Peter Lougheed Provincial Park, Height of the Rockies Provincial Park, and Banff National Park—Palliser Falls, Palliser Pass, Palliser River, not to mention Kananaskis itself, an anglicized approximation of a name Palliser heard the Stoney using. The exact route of his travels remains obscure, because his personal papers were destroyed in a house fire in 1923, and because the astronomical "fixes" and elevations he and his companions calculated for their reports, and used on their map, are inaccurate and misleading. Their instruments had given them trouble from the moment they disembarked in New York. Eventually, both barometers burst and they wrote of the "unsteadyness" of the chronometers (barometers were used to calculate elevation while chronometers were used for the calculation of longitude).

We knew it would be too time-consuming to try to follow Palliser everywhere he ventured, or might have ventured, and to approach the passes from all possible angles, so we settled on the regions with the most obvious potential: Elk Pass, and North and South Kananaskis Passes. Reiterating a generally accepted guess, several of our guidebooks suggested that Palliser headed west through North Kananaskis Pass, the route he recommended for a road across the mountains. Many of Palliser's descriptions fit this route and we too would have been entirely convinced apart from the fact that the many avalanche chutes in the narrow valley would severely limit winter use.

On August 22, a century and a half after Palliser camped at North Kananaskis Pass, Steve and I packed our backpacks and loaded up our truck once again. By this point in the summer, packing was becoming routine. One pair of long pants, one pair of shorts. One long-sleeved shirt, two short-sleeved shirts. Sun hat, sandals, fleece, mittens and toque, gortex raincoat, and a couple of pairs of socks. Tent, sleeping bags, thermarests, headlamps, stove, pots, bowls, cups and cutlery, water filter, first aid kit, and sunscreen.

As for food, oatmeal or other cereal for breakfast, and coffee, store-bought dehydrated meals for dinner, and for lunch crackers, nuts, peanut butter, beef jerky, landjagger sausages, and an assortment of power bars, fruit bars, and cereal bars. And, of course, several maps, guidebooks, our GPS and dictaphone, as well as pen and paper, and the dreaded camera.

We drove up the steep and winding dirt road that clings tenaciously to the side of Mount Rundle as it ascends to Whiteman's Gap—a rather obvious notch in the grey wall of mountains hemming in the Bow Valley. Once we crested the pass, the unpaved road, which eventually links up with Highway 40 in Peter Lougheed Provincial Park, levels out and follows the eastern shore of the Spray Lakes Reservoir. This long, narrow body of water appeared in 1930 when engineers diverted and dammed the Spray River for a hydro reservoir to run the coal mines and lime and gypsum pits in the Bow Valley. The remote and silently beautiful valley was once part of Banff National Park, but was removed to allow for the hydro electric development. Alberta has since designated it as a provincial park.

After about forty kilometres, the dirt road veers slightly southeast and enters Peter Lougheed Provincial Park. We were soon treated to a grand, sweeping panorama of slanting, knife-edge, grey walls rising above two jewel-like lakes, the Upper and Lower Kananaskis Lakes, bounded by lumpy glacier-strapped rocks and ice-smothered mountains. We parked at the furthest end of the road, along the shores of Upper Kananaskis Lake—yet another lake that has been dammed and expanded to create a hydro reservoir, and now the focal point of one of the premier parks in the Canadian Rockies.

Don, fully recovered from Athabasca Pass and the Minnewanka ride, joined us again on this trip. Again, the beautiful, cloudless summer weather that we had enjoyed for several weeks began to dissipate. Ill-looking clouds brooded above the mountain tops and a chilly wind crept down from the glaciers. "Looks like you've cursed me with bad weather again," Don announced. I laughed, but didn't bother to point out that the only consistent component of the bad weather equation this summer was Don himself. Steve and I had enjoyed glorious weather on the trips we had done alone, but were never so entertained as when we were in Don's company.

Our plan was to hike into a campground called The Forks, situated where the trails to South and North Kananaskis Passes separated, and from there launch out on a long counter-clockwise loop up over the North Pass, and then descend toward the Palliser River. We would follow the river for a few kilometres, skirting the base of Mount Beatty, and return to camp via the South Pass. This trip could also be done as an overnight excursion, but because we had heard disturbing reports about the state of the trail on the British Columbia side in Height of the Rockies Provincial Park, we wanted to travel light in case we had to bushwhack. As we had discovered over the course of the summer, going overland is a

Porcupine near The Forks.

masochistic exercise, particularly when one is burdened with the weight of a full backpack. If we were going to break our earlier pact of no more bushwhacking, it would only be for a lightly burdened day hiking adventure.

We got a very late start. By the time we finished loading our packs, it was around seven PM. We set off at a quick pace for The Forks, seven kilometres away. Even at our relatively quick rate, it would take almost two hours, and we didn't want to set up camp in the dark. Don had brought a bottle of wine to celebrate leaving his old job, and starting another, and since there was a fire ban over the entire region, he wanted to be able to crack it before dark. "I want to commemorate my retirement," he said, "however short-lived." We hiked in silence, skirting the shore of the lake before entering the forest. After several kilometres, we came unmistakably upon the jumbled, chaotic, boulder-strewn slope that Palliser wrote about in his Journal. Some dark, ominous clouds were brewing over the highest peaks in the direct line of our trail.

We arrived at the camp just as darkness settled over the mountains. It had been an uneventful walk, although we did encounter several spruce grouse and several porcupines. The grouse just stood in the middle of the trail, perhaps believing they were camouflaged, until we poked them with our hiking poles or walked too close, at which point they furiously burst into action, flapping and wheezing as they lumbered gracelessly ten metres or so before settling down again, sometimes on a spruce branch. The porcupines were strange and curious creatures, though friendly enough. Only after we almost stumbled upon them would they lumber ponderously into the bush, their rear spines raised to ward off danger, and then painstakingly creep up a tree, observing us with curious eyes in friendly faces.

After we set up our tents, we wandered over to a central eating area for a snack, to toast Don's temporary retirement. Because we were only seven kilometres from the trailhead at this camp, and we planned on making it our base camp for a couple of days, venturing forth to explore the region on lengthy day hikes, we had packed a few luxuries normally, and sadly, absent from most of our backcountry trips: wine, cheese, bread, and apples. Only one other person shared the campsite, a young fellow from southern Ontario named Tim, and his dog Bear. As darkness crept over the camp, Tim told us of his extended trip to the Rockies, and we gave him several suggestions on where to find the best scenery and the most rewarding backpacking. Without a fire, we turned in early.

When we crawled out of our warm sleeping bags for breakfast, Tim was stamping around the clearing looking uncomfortable. Apparently, he had nearly "froze his ass off" the night before. "What kind of sleeping bag do you have?" Steve asked. He delved into his tiny one person tent and dragged out a sad, droopy, and woefully small bag with a bold label pronouncing that it weighed only one pound. "Well," Don said, as diplomatically as he could. "That's one pound better than nothing, I guess."

"But it's mid-August," Tim said, exasperated. Obviously, he was used to Ontario's warmer weather. I was dressed in lightweight pants, a fleece jacket, mittens and a toque, as were Don and Steve—standard clothing year-round at higher elevations in the mountains. It's nothing to brag about, but in the high country, poor weather and freezing nights are normal every month of the year. I remember one backcountry trip in mid-August when my water bottle froze solid in my tent overnight. There is no summer camping up here. Tim promised he would get a better bag before attempting the more ambitious hikes we had suggested the night before.

An hour later, it was pleasantly warm, despite the clouds, and we were savouring the last mouthfuls of coffee, ground only the day before and freshly brewed. No sense in roughing it too much!

During breakfast, Tim confirmed my fears about our planned day hike. Alberta park rangers had dissuaded him from attempting our intended route. The trail was apparently grown over and difficult to find. We decided to attempt it, but agreed to return from the North Pass if the weather looked poor, a round trip distance of only twenty kilometres. A few weeks earlier, Steve and I had been up near South Kananaskis Pass on a day trip with some friends—a lengthy thirty-five kilometre day hike over Northover Ridge that could also have been enjoyed as a beautiful backpacking trip. From the Ridge, we had a clear view of the South Kananaskis Pass and the entire Palliser River Valley, as well as the Royal Group that forms the western ridge of the valley. Neither of us had ever been to North Kananaskis Pass, however, and the thought of reaching new scenery spurred us on.

We lunged up the trail, nearly jogging, so free did it feel to be hiking without a heavy pack. After following beside the burbling waters of the Upper Kananaskis River, we turned uphill and ascended across an avalanche chute. The valley was narrow and

On the forest floor.

steep, bounded on the far east side by the lofty limestone wall of the Spray Mountains, grey upturned slabs of an ancient sea bed, all jagged and pointy. Above us, we could see the steep, sparsely vegetated rock of Mount Putnik and Mount Beatty. Judging by the great swath of dead trees and stunted bushes, terrible avalanches had roared each year from this side of the valley, washing over the frozen river and tearing up the other side. It didn't take much imagination to realize the fate of a rail line or road built in the valley bottom. Staring down the valley behind me, in the southeastern sky I could see two large outcroppings, sparsely vegetated, with a small glacier wedged between the two largest peaks. A shimmering stream and waterfall carried the meltwater into the river near our camp below. It was a grand and wild scene, ominous amidst the terrible destruction wrought by the avalanches.

The trail then entered the secluded glades of an ancient larch forest before emerging onto a stony and barren plateau, with grey spires jutting into the sky, boulders strewn around the shores of shallow, broad, alpine lakes. At a campground named Turbine Canyon for the narrow gorge through which Maude Brook plunges with incredible force into the Upper Kananaskis River, the weather lurched closer toward what Don

The stony and barren plateau en route to North Kananaskis Pass.

jokingly classified as "disagreeable." We decided to quickly push on to the pass, another two kilometres distant, before the storm worsened. After about twenty minutes, we were assaulted by a blast of freezing wind and hail. Tenacious wildflowers bent and buckled, but I vowed to at least get a view into the Palliser River valley before admitting defeat and retracing my steps to camp. Even though I was the one most weary of bushwhacking, I hate leaving a project undone. It just bugs me, and I was not yet prepared to admit that we had to turn around.

We followed the shore of windswept Maude Lake, watching a great, dirty, polar blue glacier to the south. At the lip of the pass, I could see a winding path descending precipitously into BC before disappearing entirely amongst the stunted spruce and fir and rocks. Still, I was tempted. The elevation of the pass was 2,370 metres, providing for a very short snow-free season. If indeed this was the route Palliser described in his Journal, it would be easy to imagine his party spending a "chill and uncomfortable night" here.

"Should we avoid death, or provoke it?" Don asked. The freezing rain slackened a little, and I was even more tempted to push on, but given the absence of a clearly defined trail, and the horrible weather, I knew it was foolish. Steve and Don wisely agreed. We returned from the stark, brooding barrens of the pass to the relative shelter of the Turbine campground, and made a detour to inspect the canyon.

Leaving the gorge, we descended as quickly as possible to our camp and changed into drier clothes. After a meal, we brewed up some tea and sat on the logs that encircled a large firepit. A huge pile of perfectly chopped wood was stacked nearby under some trees. We honoured the fire ban even though it was drizzling, forlornly staring at the cold and damp firepit.

"It's just not the same, is it?" Don sighed, shifting his hands into his pockets to stay warm.

"I feel like I'm watching one of those plastic TVs in a furniture store, waiting for the scene to change," I said.

Pages 146–147: In the wind and rain near Lawson Lake.

Steve rummaged in his coat pocket and pulled out a pack of matches. He defiantly lit one and tossed it into the pit. We silently watched it sputter and go out. It was about nine PM, and it was too cold to stay outside so we crawled into our tents. The next morning, we reluctantly got up and brewed extra coffee and lingered for an hour before packing up. The weather remained neutral, not particularly inspiring, and we did not linger long before hiking out and heading back to Canmore. This trip seemed disappointing; perhaps we were all worn out from our summer of travel, or perhaps it was the dismal weather. Nonetheless, I felt no obligation to manufacture a "crisis" or create an unnecessary challenge for myself.

Certainly the North and South Kananaskis Passes did not look welcoming for either a highway or a railway. If one had been built here, it probably would have been a star attraction for tourists searching for the greatest bungled mega-project in Canadian history, or perhaps it would have become known for its sensational rail disasters. The treacherous Kicking Horse Pass looks tame and plausible compared to these rugged ascents and descents. It is hard to imagine someone as reasonable and practical as John Palliser proposing a road or rail route over either North or South Kananaskis Pass. We didn't have to read very far to discover that many others have come to the same conclusion, suggesting several different alternatives for his proposed route. The most likely of these is Elk Pass, the low broad valley in the same vicinity as the Kananaskis Passes, but leading south, not west.

Palliser's calculations of elevation are very close to the elevation of the mellow Elk Pass, at around 1,900 metres, and his descriptions could be made to fit. Perhaps Elk Pass was the route which he recommended for a road to solidify British claims to western North America—although one wonders why he was so evasive in his descriptions. Historians have suggested that one of the reasons (in addition to insider land speculation) the eventual rail route was built at great expense and seemingly against common sense over Kicking Horse Pass in today's Yoho National Park was because of fears that the southern terminus of Elk Pass would have come too close to the American border. In the years following the Oregon boundary dispute, which eventually culminated in 1846 in the establishment of the border west of the Continental Divide along the 49th parallel, Britain had good reason to anticipate American encroachment into British Columbia and southern Alberta. For military and logistical reasons, a road or railway that could be easily captured by American troops would be a waste of money, and perhaps even an enticement to the expanding southern republic.

We had ventured over Elk Pass and West Elk Pass earlier in the summer. As it was located at a much lower elevation than the other passes we planned to hike, we were able to set off earlier in the season, when most other mountain passes remained plugged with snow. Back in mid-June, we were anxious to get on the trail, even if it meant beginning our trips out of sequence. June 17 was a day of mixed sun and cloud. As we drove south we tried to spot the pass—usually, from our experience, a daunting, malevolent, gloomy, and nearly impassable notch in an unbroken line of jagged stone bordered by sheer rock walls and capped by forbidding glaciers. Such is the nature of the Rocky Mountains. But I was stunned as we approached what appeared to be a low, forested hill bordered by large, imposing mountains on either side, heading south, not west. Could this indeed be the pass that Palliser originally called Kananaskis and that was heralded as the obvious route through the mountains?

To the west, we could clearly see the bewildering and inaccessible crags that led to North and South Kananaskis Passes. Our map showed, shockingly, only ten kilometres

Looking south down the Elk Valley.

separating our parking lot from a parking lot for Elk Lakes Provincial Park in BC at the end of the long and rough Elk River Forest Service Road. For ecological reasons, a road had never been built connecting the Kananaskis Valley to the Elk Valley, despite the desires of the town of Elkford further south along the Elk Valley. The town would benefit greatly from the increased tourism.

We greeted Steve's uncle Ron, and his two kids Jonathan and Michelle, who we had invited to join us for part of the day's hike. They planned to turn around after lunch, while we continued into BC. Dutifully, they had brought raincoats and packed lunches, unlike on previous trips when they conveniently forgot water and food and ate and drank ours at an alarming speed until we had to impose rationing. While standing around, we wandered over to the trailhead and read a newly posted sign warning of a grizzly bear wandering in the region.

"No problem for us, though," Ron casually mentioned, as we booted up in the parking lot. "Grizzlies always eat the smallest first." Michelle and Jonathan laughed, but we noticed that the diminutive Jonathan, only eleven years old, quietly grabbed a larger day pack, even after we reassured him that grizzlies eat roots and grasses and rarely stalk humans for food.

We marched up through a mixed pine and spruce forest typical of Alberta's mountains, until we crossed beneath a power line heading roughly in the same direction as the pass. The trails were a series of fire roads and hydro line clearings. It would have been easy to build a road here, were it not for the fact that two provincial parks have jurisdiction over the area. I was quietly thankful that no road would be built here—the wilderness is already carved into enough pieces by other thoroughfares.

The trail was wet and loamy, heady with spicy scents after the recent rains of June, the wettest month in the Rockies. On both sides, we noticed recent signs of grizzlies diggings for roots and bulbs, some half-eaten with the fang marks still visible, and fresh bear dung scattered along the trail. The trail headed into a ravine with reasonably steep sides before widening onto a flat plain after a short climb. The five of us continued past several marshy beaver-dam-flooded clearings. The trees were like black macabre skeletons, clutching up toward the sky, with stringy moss dangling from their outstretched appendages, intriguing in their death. After about four short kilometres, we emerged into a broader clearing where we could see snow-dusted peaks on either side of the pass.

We had reached the Alberta–BC border faster than expected. The alpine meadow was covered in glacier lilies and wild crocuses (anemones) and, from our vantage point the flat grey stone of the Elk Range ran like a wall south as far as we could see, precisely mirroring Palliser's cryptic description. The Elk Valley is a narrow north–south confine with no possible exit east or west for over one hundred kilometres, a flat sheet of solid rock, striated with ice and snow like a knife-edge. Palliser probably led his horse brigade right down the middle of the flat meadows. Without the well-maintained provincial park hiking trails, it would have been very hard going here without horses, as the ground was marshy and wet—a tangled latticework of detritus. As it was, though, on the worst portions, we casually strolled along a wooden boardwalk elevated above the marsh, and the trail in the forest was cleared of debris and deadfall.

"Wouldn't it be easier to do this trip on horseback?" queried twelve-year-old Michelle, who loves horses and, among many other dreams, hopes to live on a ranch in the foothills someday.

Steve told her that Palliser, and almost all the early explorers and travellers, travelled by horse and hunted for most of their food.

"Cool," she said.

We stopped for lunch at spooky looking Fox Lake, with a great ring of withered, white skeletal trees surrounding it, and a stone amphitheatre rising above, concealing from view the appropriately named higher elevation Frozen Lake. Lunch was quick because of the cold wind. Ron, Jonathan, and Michelle headed back to their car, and Steve and I continued on alone, along this approximation of Palliser's route. We emerged from the forest onto an avalanche chute to see a beautiful green lake below us and the broad Elk Valley running south. Flat and level, this valley would be the obvious choice of someone searching for a route through the mountains. Like we had been on Howse Pass, here we were easily led along a path of little resistance, over the Great Divide.

We descended to our camp along the shore of Lower Elk Lake. The water shimmered on the cliff faces, in places exploding off rocks and shooting from caverns, glowing in the evening sun. The Upper Lake was a beautiful sheet of turquoise, with a massive deadfall dam where the river plunged through to the Lower Lake. The mounds of grey trees looked like rib cages of ancient, bleached bones—a mounded ossuary plugging the outflow of the lake, or a lost graveyard of the mammoths. If a road were ever built here,

On the trail to Elk Lakes.

there would no doubt be a huge hotel on the shores of one or both of these lakes, and a golf course carved out of the surrounding forest.

After a snack, we wandered the shores of the lakes in the early evening, imagining where Palliser might have gone. Along the banks of a river swollen with meltwater, we spied a fat porcupine burrowing in the ashes of an old campfirepit. It raised its spines in a defensive ring before scrambling up a tree, from which it observed us curiously. At first I felt guilty for frightening it, but then observed it contentedly munching on new spring shoots while keeping an eye on us. We continued along a trail up a west-leading gravel-strewn valley, but it became quickly apparent that it was a dead end, blocked by massive rock walls and granite spires soaring up in all directions.

Back at our camp, the glowing sunset clouds became ominously dark as we prepared a quick dinner of dehydrated maple beans. It began to rain before we finished eating. Hastily, we scrambled under the sheltering boughs of a shaggy spruce before slinking into our tent for the night. The next morning, was cold and damp and we lingered in bed during periodic showers before reluctantly dressing for what promised to be an uncomfortable and wet day. In the morning, my hands almost froze lowering and untying our food from the bear pole, where it had dangled like a colourful and enticing pinata the entire night. Low-lying mist hovered about the peaks, blocking all vision of the mountains or the pass. Clouds of mist drifted across the lake, and everything was still. As Steve filtered water along the shore, he was graced with the sight of a baby moose in the grasses across an inlet, before the gangly mother emerged from the reeds, noticed him, and led her offspring into the sheltering forest.

We made hot cereal and coffee to counter the dampness and chill, and huddled under the same spruce that had sheltered us the night before. While we were eating it started to rain, and we packed up quickly, finishing our coffee in the drizzle. Little did we know, we would spend many more wet and chilly mornings before the summer was over. In the steady downpour, we reconsidered our plan, and decided to return to our truck instead of exploring the park more thoroughly. Freezing rain, we concluded, was not inspiring our curiosity. We decided to return via West Elk Pass, along the marshy valley floor, the route Palliser probably would have travelled. A road would now exist there but for the whimsical fate of history. Fog enshrouded the mountains, geese flew overhead, and we trudged along a muddy trail through the woods that, judging by the hoofprints, the night before had been travelled by several large elk.

As we slogged up a small hill toward the Alberta boundary, we weren't pestered by a single insect—perhaps the only positive side effect of the declining temperatures. As we crested the hill, the land became silent and the rain became heavier and finally collected on our packs and on the ground as sticky snow. It was here that we stumbled upon a set of huge, fresh grizzly prints in the muck. The bear's back footprint was twice the length of a hand and was sunk two inches into the mud, with prominent claw marks poking holes in the earth an alarming distance in front of the toes. The earth surrounding the trail was torn to shreds and flung about. Not being experts in tracking, we couldn't determine the exact age of the prints, but they were fresh, perhaps only a few hours old. Perhaps only a few minutes. For the next three kilometres, we encountered several more sets of bear prints, and mounds of recently deposited bright green springtime scat. It was an indescribable feeling to know that I was not in terrain dominated by humans, but in terrain where wild creatures and potential accidents were my primary concern, where no phone call could bring help, and where the rules of behaviour were not established. I was filled with anticipation for the summer of adventure that lay ahead.

The beautiful shore of Lower Elk Lake.

We pushed on through the increasing storm, lost in our thoughts and shivering in the winter-like conditions of mid-June. Dark sky pressed down on us and our breath came in cold clouds. Occasionally, Steve or I slipped in the mud. Later, Steve dislodged from a swaying branch a clump of heavy snow that fell on his head and slid down his back. I laughed cruelly. In the mountains, I well knew, we could expect snow every month of the year and we had to be prepared for it—but it was still a shock. By the time we reached the parking lot, the ground and our vehicle were completely covered, as if it were March or early April. We changed into dry clothes, brushed off the windshield, turned on the heater, and drove the muddy track of the Spray back to Canmore. The oppressive clouds broke as we drove north, and by the time we were descending into the Bow Valley the sun was hot and the sky blue. People rode bikes and walked dogs, gardeners planted flowers, and joggers all wore shorts. The storm clouds still hovered behind us, but in Canmore, one valley and not quite a hundred kilometres distant, it had been a beautiful warm day. And to us, that was the greatest mystery of all.

As I relaxed on our deck later that evening, I heard the unmistakable rumble of a locomotive rolling west down the Bow Valley, headed toward Lake Louise and then down Hector's Kicking Horse Pass. It was a tangible reminder of how things had changed since Palliser's rudimentary explorations—the railway and roads were no longer a dream of the British Colonial Office, but part of the commonplace infrastructure of trade and travel. It took more than twenty-five years after Palliser's expedition before the railway finally pushed its way over the Continental Divide. The trains changed the land forever, for the first time opening the mountains to a different type of explorer.

Part Four
FOLLOWING MARY SCHÄFFER

Chapter Nine

MOUNTAIN WOMAN AND A MYTHICAL LAKE

With the construction of the Canadian Pacific Railway through the Rockies in 1886, and with the new Canadian government and CPR actively seeking to promote a British presence in the western mountains, the lure to explore this wild land was irresistible to wealthy eccentrics. Just after the turn of the century, Mary Schäffer, a Philadelphia Quaker, began a long association with Canada's mountain wilderness. Several years after the death of her first husband in 1903, she threw aside the shackles of social propriety and did the unthinkable for a woman at the time—she became a wilderness explorer.

Over several years, she and several others, including guide and future husband Billy Warren, ventured into many unknown valleys on horseback and pioneered a route to the now famous Maligne Lake in Jasper National Park. Unlike many of the other wanderers who traversed the mountains in the past, including Palliser, Simpson, and Thompson, Schäffer pursued no commercial or political objectives. She travelled for her own pleasure and peace of mind—and eventually under the auspices of the fledgling conservation movement then fighting to secure the National Parks as protected places. The Stoney people recognized her as a unique species of traveller, eventually naming her *Yahe-Weha*—mountain woman.

Schäffer was not the typical wealthy gentlewoman of the time. Despite a fear of horses and bears, and recurring bouts with neuralgia, an intermittent but painful nerve disorder, she evolved from a pampered and charming socialite to a competent and knowledgeable woodswoman, comfortable in the wilderness for months on end. Her first experience camping with horses in 1893 was an indication of how much she

Looking east toward the Brazeau Valley.

changed in the following years. Looking out from her tent "upon that magnificent scene, with chattering teeth and shivering bodies," she wrote, "I vowed never again to camp in the Canadian Rockies."

Years later, however, when she was well-known for her wilderness escapades, after the publication of her classic book of mountain exploration *Old Indian Trails of the Canadian Rockies*, Schäffer's opinion of life in the wild had changed dramatically. "We have passed weeks of showery or snowy days in the hills," she claimed proudly, and "never knew ourselves to catch cold, and on taking everything into account could only conclude that nature meant us all to be wild flowers instead of house-plants." She also wrote of her sorrow when returning to civilization. "It was then," she wrote, "that I wanted my wild free life back again, yet step by step I was leaving it behind."

On one occasion, in August 1907, she was leading her horse back toward Mount Stephen House, along the route of the railroad in Yoho National Park, when she encountered Rudyard Kipling who was touring the shores of Emerald Lake. "As we drove along the narrow hill road," Kipling condescendingly wrote in *Letters of Travel 1892–1913*, "a piebald pack-pony with a china-blue eye came round a bend, followed by two women, black-haired, bare-headed, wearing beadwork squaw jackets and riding straddle. . . . 'Indians on the move?' said I. 'How characteristic!' As the women jolted by, one of them very slightly turned her eyes, and they were, past any doubt, the comprehending equal eyes of the civilized white woman which moved in that berry-brown face. 'Yes,' said our driver . . . 'they mostly camp here-a-bout for three months every year. I reckon they're coming in to the railroad before the snow falls.' That same evening, in a hotel of all the luxuries, a slight woman in a very pretty evening frock was turning over photographs, and the eyes beneath the strictly arranged hair were the eyes of the woman in the beadwork jacket."

Mary Townsend Sharples was born to a wealthy Quaker family in West Chester, Philadelphia, on October 4, 1861, just a year after John Palliser returned from his expedition to the southern Rockies. Highly educated in the Quaker tradition, in natural history, mathematics, literature, and painting, her early life revolved around the cultured society and drawing rooms of Philadelphia. At an early age she developed an intense curiosity about the native peoples of the continent, and on several family trips to the American west went out of her way to meet the original inhabitants of the land. An 1889 trip from Montreal to Vancouver aboard the new Canadian Pacific Railway changed her life forever. At Glacier House, the railroad's new hotel in Roger's Pass, she was introduced to Dr. Charles Schäffer, a wealthy Philadelphia doctor twenty-three years her senior who had an intense interest in botany. In Philadelphia, they renewed their acquaintance and were soon married, planning another trip to the Canadian Rockies in 1891.

For twelve years, they returned each summer to collect botanical specimens, and although they seldom strayed far from the rail line or rude roads and well-trodden horse tracks, for Schäffer these excursions were a timid introduction to the wilderness she would come to love. Her much older husband suffered from heart problems, which limited their excursions, so apart from an occasional trip into the woods, they stayed in the luxury of the CPR hotels in Banff, Laggan Station (Lake Louise), Stephen House (Field), and Glacier. While her husband worked on a book of the flora of the Canadian Rockies, Schäffer also took an interest and began to draw and paint the specimens to illustrate the book.

Mary Schäffer at camp, 1907.

1903 was a brutal year for her. In the fall, Schäffer's husband and both her parents died. Their deaths coincided with a crash in the stock markets (and the loss of a considerable amount of the family fortune) and Schäffer was left with a desire to return to the mountains to complete her husband's book. With the help of a prominent Philadelphia naturalist, she was able to do so. She hired a young guide named Billy Warren and spent the next several years probing deeper into the wilds, while collecting plant specimens with several female

Philadelphia friends. Her book, *Alpine Flora of the Canadian Rockies*, was published in 1907, and its completion seemed to release her from following in her husband's footsteps.

As her trail skills improved, so did her desire to venture further afield. In 1907, the year Jasper Park was created, Schäffer and her companion Mollie Adams, a New York geology teacher, planned an ambitious expedition into the wilds, against the advice and concerns of their families and social peers in the east. A wilderness expedition was not considered appropriate for women of their social background. At forty-six, Schäffer was expected to be matronly and domestic rather than daring and adventurous. But "why not?" she asked. "We can starve as well as they; the muskeg will be no softer for us than for them; the ground will be no harder to sleep upon; the waters no deeper to swim, nor the bath colder if we fall in."

Schäffer, Adams, and two guides, Warren and Sid Unwin, set out with a pack train of horses in late June to "penetrate to the head waters of the Saskatchewan and Athabasca rivers." During the three month season, they followed the old Indian trails over Bow Pass, along the North Saskatchewan River to Brazeau Lake and Fortress Lake before returning over Howse Pass to Field. A chance encounter in September at Saskatchewan Crossing, near the spot where David Thompson had waited impatiently for the snow to melt a century earlier, gave Schäffer her first concrete evidence of a mysterious lake called *Chaba Imne*, Beaver Lake, that was rumoured to lie somewhere north of Brazeau Lake. A Stoney named Sampson Beaver related how he had been there in his youth and scrawled a rough map for Shäffer—"a tiny grubby bit of paper" where "a very scribbly spot was a pass" and "something which looked like a squashed spider [was] a mountain." They failed to find the fabled lake in 1907, but spent the winter of 1907 to 1908 planning an expedition there. Although pleasure and just being in the wilderness were her main objectives, the rediscovery of the mythical lake provided a greater sense of purpose to her wanderings.

"In the spring of 1908," she wrote "a small party of six . . . unnoticed by a solitary soul, slipped quietly away from civilisation and were lost, so far as the world was concerned, in a sea of mountains to the north. Our quest was a mythical lake spoken of by the Stoney Indians." The Stoney and the Cree knew of the lake but had stopped visiting it when the beavers had been hunted. And, in 1875, a Canadian Pacific Railway surveyor named Henry MacLeod had dismissed the lake and valley as unsuitable for a railroad. It was possible that the lake hadn't seen visitors in decades. In addition to Warren and Unwin and her friend Adams, Schäffer had invited the naturalist Stewardson Brown, and his assistant and guide Reggie Holmes, on their quest.

Schäffer and her entourage, and perhaps a dozen horses departed Laggan Station in June, after a spring that "crept by like a snail." They headed north over Bow Pass to Saskatchewan Crossing, and then proceeded up toward Parker Camp just south of the Columbia Icefield. From here, the pack train wound its way up and over boulder-strewn Nigel Pass and descended into the Brazeau River valley. From a windswept promontory perched over Brazeau Lake, they spied "a gap in the hills west of the lake" that was probably the pass they were searching for according to Sampson's crude map. For several days, they struggled through the dense forests along the shore of the lake on a faintly discernible trail that was covered in deadfall and scrub. They led their horses past many sites of native encampments, evident from the teepee rings and firepits. It was hard going. Poboktan Pass was "fierce," with "quick changes from burnt timber to rock climbing, muskeg, quicksand, scree slopes and mud slides." The drizzly weather and uncertain route weighed heavily upon them. "There was an absence of joking," she recalled, "there was no whistling in front or warbling of the latest popular song in the rear."

Through the snow, almost a metre deep, and spongy muskegs, the horses laboured, climbing ever upward out of the forest and into a broad, alpine valley that stretched away to the north and west. "It was a hard climb up and over," she wrote, "and now that I have seen it I should never take the Poboktan Pass from start to finish for a pleasure trip; it is a miserable route, and one only to be used to accomplish an end." The cavalcade crept down from the pass in early July and began heading along the east shore of Poboktan Creek. According to Sampson's map, they were to leave this valley "at the third creek coming in from the right," but she noted with exasperation that they had already passed about a dozen creeks, swollen with meltwater, and it was hard to keep their bearings. As a mirror to their thoughts, they "could see the sun just setting in a bank of angry clouds, the wind, which had not been any too pleasant all day, began to howl and sob."

The next morning, July 4, "it took a terrible lot of courage to emerge from the warm blankets, from which position we noted six inches of snow over everything." The travellers huddled about the smouldering fire and drank their coffee barely warm. The bacon was "like candle-grease." They miserably packed up camp and set off down "a fire swept valley" where the axes were out constantly, chopping deadfall from the trail. They came upon another teepee ring and a branch in the faint trail, one fork leading west into the Sunwapta Valley, the other angling "into a notch in the hills with a northern trend." The weary group slowly scrambled through the brush until Warren, tiring of the snail-like progress, set off alone to inspect the route. He rejoined the party several hours later claiming to have found a good trail leading up through a pass and into a forested valley—but not to a lake. From the crest of the pass, now known as Maligne Pass, they hastily descended to the valley bottom, where they spent the night again at an old encampment.

There was still no sign of the mythical lake as they rode through the grasses at the river's edge. "We certainly looked our thoughts," Schäffer recorded, "and rode along in dead silence." The scenery, however, was magnificent. The valley was blooming, with a great "mass of forget-me-nots, great splashes of intense blue, as though a bit of the sky had fallen." After stopping for a break in the early afternoon, Unwin, increasingly impatient and anxious, announced he was setting off alone to climb a nearby mountain and "see if that lake's within twenty miles of here, and I'm not coming back until I know." The remaining five waited out the afternoon and evening "tormented by hordes of mosquitoes" and their own fears. When the sun had set, and darkness crept over the land, they made a "rousing" fire as a beacon to Unwin. He didn't return until 10:30 PM, exhausted and hungry, but elated as he announced, "I've found the lake!"

The next morning, the excited troupe rose, ate a hasty breakfast, and led the horses along the overgrown trail for about two hours, until they emerged from the woods, wandered out onto a gravel beach, and beheld the vast expanse of Maligne Lake stretching far down the valley, north and south. "As we stood upon its shores," Schäffer wrote, "we looked across to the other side, wondered what it all held in store for us, then wandered around while the men looked for a good campsite." Again, they chose a spot used by unknown indigenous people in the past—a clearing, a little back from the lakeshore, that was grown over with grasses for the horses. The next day, they began the construction of a large raft to explore the lake—the extensive deadfall would have made it very tiring and slow to lead the pack horses along the shore. After a long day of labour, the HMS *Chaba* was lake worthy, and the next morning they began loading the precarious craft, preparing for a journey of several days.

The camp at Maligne Lake, 1908.

Despite "sensations towards large bodies of water similar to those of a cat," Schäffer and Adams with "qualms and misgivings" allowed themselves to be ignominiously carried out to the raft like pieces of baggage. The raft was a crude, overloaded conglomerate of green logs that ponderously swayed with the waves, with water fully washing the floor when someone shifted position. They poled the "clumsy little craft, foot by foot, past exquisite bays and inlets," as they worked their way to what they assumed was the head of the lake in the south. What they supposed to be the southern shore, however, was really only a narrowing of the lake that led to an even grander spectacle. "There burst upon us," Schäffer wrote, "that which, all in our little company agreed, was the finest view any of us had ever beheld in the Rockies." They had reached the narrows of the lake, clearly drawn on Sampson's map, yet scarcely visible until they were upon it. The lake was much larger than they had hoped for—"those miles and miles of lake, the unnamed peaks rising above us, one following the other, each more beautiful than the last."

As they rafted the perimeter of the great lake, they named many of the nearby mountains after themselves and their friends: Mount Unwin, The Thumb, Mount

Warren, Mount Mary Vaux, Sampson's Peak. "How pure and undefiled it was! We searched for some sign that others had been there, not a teepee-pole, not a charred stick, not even tracks of game; just masses of flowers, the lap-lap of the waters on the shore, the occasional reverberating roar of an avalanche, and our own voices, stilled by a nameless Presence." Several days later, on July 12, they returned to their original camp, named Camp Unwin, "thus ending probably the first voyage ever taken on Maligne Lake." Today, boat tours take people from the north end of the lake, where the road from Jasper ends, to the narrows, to behold the solemn, undisturbed wilderness of the southern portion of the lake.

After a miserable night fending off swarms of mosquitoes, the six travellers began preparing for a jaunt to the north end of the lake on horseback. They set off on "an old Indian trail" through the woods, and by the day's end had arrived at the lake's northern shore, where they set up camp adjacent to the Maligne River. Schäffer and her companions decided to follow the Maligne River northwest to link up with the Yellowhead Trail toward Mount Robson, the highest mountain in the Canadian Rockies. After a restful evening along the shores of the river they learned why the river was named Maligne, French for wicked. As Unwin drove his horse into the shallow, fast flowing water, he was surprised when it suddenly rose to saddle height and his horse "turn[ed] over backwards." Washed from the saddle, Unwin began swimming furiously against the current to reach the shore. The horse "with head under and feet up, [was] being borne quickly towards the rapids only a hundred yards below." Luckily, they both managed to scramble to safety in time.

The next day, they built another "bulky old raft" and ferried themselves across while the horses swam unburdened. It took several trips, and most of the day, before they were safely on the other bank. They then devoted themselves to searching for a trail north "thirty miles at the most" toward the Athabasca River, but "at every turn we were met with burnt timber, ravines, and insurmountable walls of rock, till, after six hours trudging, we turned back weary and discouraged." On July 20, they began chopping their way through a "fearful amount of down-timber." Conditions did not improve as they neared Medicine Lake, but Schäffer and Adams were glad for a rest and some privacy when the men departed in the morning leaving "not a soul to pry into our domestic efforts!"

A falen log across the trail.

After five days of cutting, they realized the direct route to the Athabasca River would be far too clogged and difficult for the horses, so they abandoned it and unceremoniously retreated back over Maligne Pass, bidding "farewell to the only kingdom we could call our own." They were so exhausted by the time they reached the Sunwapta Valley that Brown, the botanist, and his assistant and nine horses departed for home, while the remaining four continued north following the Sunwapta River to the Athabasca and then on to Mount Robson. They continued to adventure and explore until September, touring the remains of the abandoned fur trading post, Henry House, near present-day Jasper, which had been the depot for travellers crossing Athabasca Pass.

The most disturbing event of Schäffer's journey was seeing an unbroken line of white wooden stakes running west along the Athabasca River and then continuing over Yellowhead Pass. They were survey markers for the railway, carving through the heart of the wilderness. As the group retraced their route south over Bow Pass toward Laggan Station, Schäffer was struck with the realization that, with the planned Grand Trunk Pacific Railway running through the newly created Jasper Forest Park, and over the Yellowhead Pass, the mountains would never be the same. The federal government had created the park by decree in 1907 to boost tourism, but it remained unmapped, unsurveyed, and rarely, if ever, visited by tourists, because there was no access. "All would be made easy with trains and bridges," Schäffer lamented, "the hideous march of progress, so awful to those who love the real wilderness, was sweeping rapidly over the land and would wipe out all trail troubles."

Three years passed before Schäffer again returned to these mountains. During the fall and winter of 1908 to 1909, she and Adams ventured to Japan for a tour. The delightfully civilized touring, so different from their summer's adventure, was marred by tragedy. Adams died unexpectedly, leaving Schäffer without a female travelling companion. Upon her return, Schäffer began to write of her adventures in numerous magazines and newspapers, as well as in her book on her exploration in the Rockies, which was published in 1911.

She became a celebrity. She was asked by Dr. D.B. Dowling of the Geological Survey of Canada to lead a survey expedition to Maligne Lake. The lake and surrounding mountains were removed from Jasper Forest Park in 1911, when its size was shrunk from five thousand square miles to little over one thousand, mostly bordering the proposed Grand Trunk Pacific Railway. Although it was official policy not to hire women for surveying work, Dowling hoped that Schäffer's fame as a writer and explorer would attract public attention and assist efforts to reincorporate Maligne Lake within the park boundaries. Despite her initial reservations, Dowling persuaded her that she could easily learn the surveying techniques and he received funding to hire a crew to clear a trail from the Athabasca River over the mountains and down to Maligne Lake.

During the three years since Schäffer had last visited the region, great changes had occurred. Many other tourists were being guided into the backcountry. The era of discoveries was drawing to a close, and the new northern railway was bringing a wave of westward wandering pioneers. "Two summers have flooded those valleys with sunshine," she wrote, "three winters have choked them with snow, but nothing has held back the tide of 'improvement' foretold by the harmless-looking line of white pegs [survey markers], and many are those who rejoice in the fact. Not so ourselves. With every mile over which we hear the 'python' has worked his way still further into the hills comes a fresh pang of regret that, inch by inch, our pet playgrounds are being swallowed up. . . . With all the time and seasons fled, however, there still lived in my mind the memory of the beautiful lake and an ever increasing desire to see it once more before it too fell under the fatal breath of 'improvement.'"

Schäffer, her sister-in-law Caroline, and nephew Paul rode the train to Edmonton, where they were astonished to find a "mass of unnumbered nationalities" crowding the bustling streets. After several days waiting for a lost trunk, they set out by rail for the frontier. The train took them as far as the temporary boom town of Prairie Creek, near present-day Hinton, where they met their two guides, Unwin and Jack Otto, who led them to a teepee on the edge of town, saving them from the discomfort of a ramshackle hotel. From then on, they rode horses, which was a much preferred mode of travel to Schäffer. But they were nowhere near wilderness. The muddy, rutted track heading west was cleared for the railway and thousands of pioneers driving their heavily loaded carts clogged the trail. "We started forth," she remembered, "occasionally passing heavily loaded freight wagons whose every plank groaned and rebelled under its load; passed a Cree village where, when we tried to photograph the untidy spot, the inhabitants scuttled like rabbits to their holes; passed abandoned construction camps; passed an isolated eating house where all the S's in the numerous signs were turned wrong way about till we wondered how anyone had mustered courage to enter there after reading them; passed along the rolling flower-decked hills on a very good road."

They spent several days following the Athabasca River into the mountains "still looking for the wilds." Perhaps the most astonishing change Schäffer witnessed was a ferry across the river, a welcome sight for most travellers. But to her, she commented, "who had stood on those banks only three years before, who had looked across that wild body of water to the fair, unbroken prairies beyond, where only the Indian trail marked the way, it was an ugly sight." They paid the fare, crossed with ease, and continued on. They camped in a clearing, now a small village, where previously no one had lived. They then led their pack train east toward Curator Mountain of the Maligne Range, beyond which lay Maligne Lake. Two huge planks of cedar were strapped onto one horse and the others carried surveying equipment and additional tools for the construction of a boat. It was a long slog, but manageable, the route having been cleared to make way for the horses. On June 17, they had ascended high enough that snow was the problem, not deadfall. Although the trail crew had tried to dig a trough, the horses struggled in the slippery, sinking, soppy mess.

Forest floor in the fall.

Far ahead, near the height of land in the pass, two dark spots were spied which Schäffer confidently claimed were sheep. As she approached "the thinnest legged sheep" she had ever seen, she "came close enough to analyze our two immovable sheep—only to find them a pair of abandoned shovels which had been hewn from a tree and, in case we needed the same, left standing conspicuously in the snow." Schäffer good-naturedly agreed the pass would be henceforth known as Shovel Pass. It still is. On June 24, they began constructing the HMS *Chaba the Second.* They spent a month at the lake, exploring nearby valleys and surveying the shores. After a few fumbles, Schäffer had no trouble completing the survey. "Beautiful? Of course it was," she wrote. With great reluctance, the small group departed on July 23, retracing their route to the railway, and returning to the outside world. "Each day," she wrote, "was a 'farewell' to some spot which for the moment had been our very own. The wedge had been driven in; in another year the secret places would be secret no more."

For the next year, Schäffer devoted her considerable energy to lobbying for Maligne Lake to be included in Jasper Park. Both the Canadian Pacific Railway and the Grand Trunk Pacific were also agitating for larger parks. The rail lines passed through some of the most spectacular alpine scenery in the world, and they wanted to maximize the tourism potential. On June 24, 1912, the boundaries of Jasper Park were expanded to again include Maligne Lake. Schäffer eventually moved from Philadelphia to Banff and married her much younger guide and travelling companion Billy Warren. She continued to write and lobby for wilderness preservation for a while, but in her later years did little travelling. She died in Banff in 1939—the same year the first road north from Lake Louise to Jasper was completed, bisecting the wilderness she had spent her later life exploring.

The coming of the railways marked the beginning of the end for the wild west. Hotels were built along the rail line and eventually roads made the mountains accessible to anyone. A map of northern Banff and southern Jasper National Park from a 1928 Department of the Interior publication bears little resemblance to a modern map of the same region. The valleys are the same, the mountains are just as high, Maligne Lake is equally as broad and deep, but there are no roads on this early map. A railway passes down the Bow Valley, with a stop at Laggan Station, and continues west over Kicking Horse Pass. A second rail line cuts Jasper Park in half, passing through Jasper and continuing west over Yellowhead Pass. The Icefields Parkway, the great winding thoroughfare connecting Jasper to the Trans-Canada Highway, is notably absent. In its place is a dotted line heading southeast from Jasper to the shores of Maligne Lake, and from the lake southwest through a series of valleys paralleling the present-day Icefields Parkway. Schäffer's original route from Lake Louise north to Maligne Lake became the well-trodden trail of horse outfitters taking tourists into the wilds, and was frequently travelled until the road was constructed. Although part of the route has now become the Icefields Parkway, over a hundred kilometres of her original trail, through terrain as stunning and wild as any in the mountain parks, is a true forgotten highway that hikers can still retrace today as a lengthy backpacking trip.

Chapter Ten
THE ABANDONED TRAIL

On September 15, we had our third Hudson's Bay start of the summer. Despite perfect weather for nearly a week, and plenty of time to plan and organize our journey, we did not set off on the trail up Nigel Pass until four PM. Our own inherent morning sluggishness was partly to blame, but so too were our travelling companions.

We had spent Thursday making last minute preparations and intending to leave, but Don begged us to wait until the weekend so that he could join us for the first leg of the journey. In spite of his terrible weather record with us, he was willing to go for it again. What were *we* thinking though? Steve's friend Chad had flown in from Vancouver two days before. The four of us met at the café in the Lake Louise International Hostel on Saturday morning, not as early as I had hoped, and we were caught at the end of the busy morning breakfast rush. Since we were already late, Don reasoned that a little extra lingering over coffee wouldn't do us any harm. "Come on, guys, poor old Don worked hard all week and needs one extra hit of caffeine."

Steve noticed my frown and interjected, "How 'bout half a cup and we'll call it a deal."

I knew the time didn't matter, in the grand scheme of things, but I am impatient by nature. I couldn't relax knowing we had to drive several hours to the trailhead, and then two more hours to drop off the truck at our end point. Don needed caffeine. I needed chamomile tea.

Steve and I had selected a route that was a collage of two of Schäffer's adventures: an approximation of her 1908 expedition to Maligne Lake and her 1911 journey to survey the lakeshore. Our plan was to head generally north toward Maligne Lake and then detour west over Shovel Pass along the Skyline Trail, before descending to a trailhead a few kilometres south of the town of Jasper.

It was a beautiful afternoon as the four of us finally set off from the Icefields

Parkway, following Nigel Creek up a broad and open valley toward Nigel Pass. It was easy to imagine the pack trains plodding along this valley; the open underbrush and plentiful meadows would have made for excellent horse travel. It was also easy to understand why the original horse trail would have been through this valley instead of the route of today's highway. Not only would the Athabasca Glacier have plugged the entire valley almost a century ago—it has been steadily retreating throughout the twentieth century and now leaves plenty of room for a road and visitor centre in the valley bottom—the bitter glacial winds and higher elevation would have shut the route for much of the year.

Fall colours tinted the landscape as we ascended Nigel Pass through shallow valleys and little depressed glades dotted with trees. The ground was swathed in burnt yellow, orange, and red willows, and dwarf birch. Stunning views of pine and spruce forest beneath grand and rocky peaks, with glaciers perched atop them shimmering against the deep blue sky, stretched in several directions. I was glad that the 1969 Parks Canada plan to build a road running from Maligne Lake through this valley was blocked by the desire to preserve the wilderness. At the summit of the pass, we found a metal rod stuck into the earth with a handwritten note scrawled on some tape covering the top. It boldly pronounced "You are here/ Vous êtes ici." It was nice to know we had arrived. Here, Chad detected a rubbing of his heels in his boots. Although an ex-Jasper Park warden and BC Parks ranger with plenty of hiking and backpacking experience to his credit, Chad had spent the last year in Japan teaching English, and he feared his feet had become soft treading nothing wilder than the urban byways of Tokyo. He was equipped with a vast array of blister-preventing paraphernalia. A good thing, as it turned out—the battle of the boot had begun.

After a brief break, we clambered down into an ancient, glacial melt chute, scrambled up the other side, and found ourselves in a blasted-looking boulder field strewn with gigantic chunks of grey rock, which seemed to have cracked off a nearby mountain and crashed down to the flat floor below. It looked, even more so than Athabasca Pass, like the valley of lost mammoths, remnants of a prehistoric era. From a rocky promontory about a kilometre further on, we peered down a long, scooped valley without trees, with a glistening braided stream winding northwest and out of sight.

Eventually, we entered a scraggly pine forest where old trees and their branches twisted chaotically, seemingly stretching out to clutch at our packs. We periodically emerged into grassy flats along the banks of the Brazeau River and several kilometres further arrived at our first camp. It was getting dark—the September sun setting so much earlier than in midsummer—so we set up our tents quickly and dragged our weighty food sacs over to the eating area and began to cook. Several other parties were in the camp, but they had already eaten and were slowly preparing for bed. By the time we were organized, the sun had set, and we finished cooking by candlelight. "Well," Don said, "since we can't see what we're about to eat, how about mixing the dehydrated meals together?" Beef stroganoff and three bean chili found themselves tossed into the same pot of boiling water. Don then sheepishly brought out a can of beans, telling us he hadn't had much time to pack. "The weight doesn't matter because I'm hiking out tomorrow," he said. And then added, "Look, at least it's Heinz . . . if you've been reduced to beans, you may as well get the brand name stuff." The can of beans also found itself heaved into the pot, and finally we ate.

It was, Don proclaimed, "a satisfying rubaboo." None of us knew what a "rubaboo" was, but we all agreed that it was one, and I later discovered we had all secretly vowed not to eat it again.

The morning was cold and shady when Steve and I crawled out of our tent. The whole valley was in shadow, with frost tingeing the trees and bushes as far as we could see. As we stood by the side of the river, filling our water bag, the sun peeked over the peak of a nearby mountain and soon the valley was awash in the weak light of morning. The frost quickly retreated, leaving wetness on the leaves and damp patches on the ground. As we huddled around the stove heating water for coffee, some nearby campers told us that their thermometer said it was minus four degrees Celsius. Smelling the coffee, Don emerged bleary eyed from his tent and joined us.

We lingered until noon in the growing warmth of a perfect fall day, then finally bade Don farewell and continued on our trek. Chad and Steve and I would temporarily veer from Schäffer's original route. While she, on horseback, had followed the Brazeau River northeast to where it flowed into Brazeau Lake, hugged the lakeshore, and then ascended Poboktan Pass, we would instead climb through Jonas Pass and then up over Jonas Shoulder before rejoining her route near Poboktan Pass. We had several reasons for this minor detour: there was reported flooding along the Brazeau Valley,

Steve, Don, Chad, and Nicky at the start of the final journey.

and the potential for some prescribed burns, and, to be entirely honest, the scenery for hikers was rumoured to be better through Jonas Pass. After a summer of slogging through dense forests, none of us could resist the temptation of spending a day in the autumn alpine. Brazeau Lake might be nice on horseback, but for a hiker it would be swampy and enclosed in dense forest. Although even ugly forest can have its appeal, an entire day slogging through uprooted trees, ill-looking marsh, partially decomposed vegetation, and oppressive shadows was more than Steve and I could bear.

It proved to be a hot day, and we were sweating in shorts and T-shirts as we crested a steep hill and emerged from the forest to behold Jonas Pass—a glorious, desolate alpine valley in green, yellow, orange, and red, with a rugged, crumbling rocky ridge running the length of it on both sides. For most of the day, we wandered between reddish boulders, crystal tarns, and burbling creeks, with a clear view of the back side of Mount Sunwapta, its snow dusted spires and glaciers strapped to its forbidding blackened crest. The land was deserted as far as we could see, and a constant warm wind

View from Jonas Shoulder.

added to the feeling of loneliness and seclusion. "I almost forgot how beautiful the mountains are," Chad said, obviously glad to have finished his tenure in the sprawling suburbs of Tokyo.

Chad's feet were surprisingly blistered from the previous day's hike, so he strolled the easy and flat trail of the pass in sandals. Fortunately, by late afternoon his blisters had receded somewhat, and he donned his hardened black boots for the rough three hundred metre climb to the top of Jonas Shoulder. The wind blew hard and cold on the Shoulder so, despite the wild beauty of the empty, curved, glacial valleys stretching away in three directions, we put our packs back over our cold, sweaty shirts and rapidly descended into the new valley. At the top, Pobokton Pass led to Brazeau Lake—where Schäffer came in 1908, and where the later horse brigades travelled—and at the bottom we found our camp for the evening, sheltered just below treeline.

The camp appeared in a clearing adjacent to a stream, just inside a copse of large spruce trees. Again, there were picnic tables at a designated eating area, a luxury we appreciated after some of our less-travelled routes. It was also a luxury to follow a well-defined trail and to have a designated, pulley-operated food hang each night. We ate a wonderfully delicious Curry-In-a-Hurry, perhaps the best dehydrated meal on the market, and lingered until after dark, listening to the water rushing by in the stream and the wind rustling the trees, and observing the final pink tendrils of a brilliant mountain sunset before heading to bed. We planned on staying here for two nights, making a day trip to the crest of nearby Poboktan Pass. We wanted to walk at least part of the terrain that we had missed, where Schäffer and the early horse brigades had passed.

We set out for the pass after breakfast, Chad again opting for sandals. The unyielding armour of his new boots had shredded his poor, soft feet leaving gaping wounds where skin should have been. The best defence against blisters, in my experience, might come as a surprise. It is that universal fixer of all things—duct tape. Chad's feet were swathed in it. As a pre-emptive strike against his boot's further assaults, he had soaked them in water, stuffed the toes full of rocks, pounded them against the ground, and carefully placed them in the sun to harden in their stretched state throughout the day. Fortunately, the trail to Poboktan Pass was dry, passing over gently rolling alpine hills on its ascent.

Near the crest of the pass, we left the trail and wandered to the top of a nearby windswept and grassy knoll, where we lounged napping in the sun for about an hour. The scenery was indescribable, and we finally departed only when I noticed that Steve was getting a serious sunburn at the high elevation. Chad observed mare's tail clouds stretching faintly across the sky, a sure sign, he claimed, of a changing weather pattern. Since the weather was perfect, and had been for some time, it boded ill for the coming days.

As we reluctantly trudged down the hill, I was struck with our good fortune as Canadians, and particularly as Canadians living near the mountain parks. In truth, very few people have the opportunity to spend time roaming over some of the earth's last remaining wild places for days at a time, to experience wilderness as it was centuries before, a wilderness that includes the trails and campsites which were probably used by various native tribes for thousands of years. It was a treat to be able to feast our eyes on untamed and unmanicured land, and to smell smells free from modern human influences. As humans, we are part of nature, yet also somehow removed from it in our sealed houses in sprawling cities—cities that are like termite hives on a grander scale. I felt as though the whole wild valley belonged to me. It would be closer to the truth, we all agreed, to say that we belonged to the place, and that's why we become attached to it.

The only thing oddly out of place was a metal rod bored into the earth, with a withered grey log nearby. The log could only have been brought there by humans at some distant time in the past, as no trees grew anywhere near the alpine highlands. As we wandered lazily down, we observed a collection of grey logs at regular intervals, more or less paralleling the trail. "Oh, those are probably the remains of the old telegraph system," Chad said, as if that were common knowledge. "The entire perimeter of the park used to be linked by a telegraph so that wardens could protect against poaching earlier in the century."

This was news to us. I later read about the mysterious Jasper telegraph. Indeed, in the 1930s the entire boundary of the park was connected by a series of poles, built over a period of years and at great expense. In the 1960s, the poles were torn down and replaced with wireless communication technology; the boundary patrol and the prevention of poaching remained important concerns for Parks Canada.

We descended from Poboktan Pass, returned to camp, and passed an untroubled and relaxed afternoon, washing our clothes in the stream and cooking up a delicious batch of Bueno Bean Stew. The rain, true to Chad's prediction, chased us into our tents at eight PM.

September 18 dawned very cold and it was only the call of nature that awoke me around seven AM. The sun had yet to creep above the nearby peaks and melt the frost that covered our tent, the ground, and all the nearby plants.

In truth, one of the most disagreeable discomforts of backpacking is putting warm feet into cold, stiff boots in the morning. When I finally got up the courage to emerge from our tent, I saw little cubes of ice frozen to the top of the fly. Steve and I shook it energetically, scattering them like tiny jewels over the ground, before we stuffed the freezing nylon into its bag. We ate breakfast standing around the frost-covered table in full winter clothes, sipping cups of steaming coffee. Another group of campers, two men from Vernon, BC, were amused to see Chad inspecting his wounded feet and re-armouring them with silver duct tape before donning his newly beaten boots. "I think I've brought them to the negotiating table," Chad said smiling, before stamping forcefully about the camp.

Hiking toward Maligne Pass.

We began the day's trek with vigour and purpose—we had twenty kilometres to go and, although the sky was blue, suspicious clouds hovered on the horizon. We wanted to get to the next camp, the curiously named Avalanche Camp, at a much higher elevation just below Maligne Pass, before rain or possibly snow soaked us and our stuff. Once the sun crested the mountains, the day became beautiful and warm and we followed a forested trail with breaks allowing views of the surrounding peaks and the sparkling Poboktan Creek. It was easy walking as we descended for two thirds of the day, before a final steep ascent to the camp. At the lower elevation, we entered berry terrain, and sure enough, as we rounded a bend in the trail, Chad spied evidence of bears. "Hello, Mr. Bear," he said, coming upon a great mound of fresh excrement, the bulk of which seemed to consist of berries and yellow leaves the same size and colour as the ones that lined the trail for the last several kilometres. The bear's footprints were smeared in the mud of the trail, revealing it to be a large black bear who had travelled for several kilometres along the same route, even using a bridge across a small stream, before vanishing.

The rain hit as we began the ascent to the camp. The clouds had been gathering

The bracing snow of September.

for about an hour, but chose to unleash their load when we were tantalizingly close to our destination. Chad stopped to pull on a raincoat, but Steve and I decided to push on and get wet, hoping that the uphill walking would keep us warm. Unfortunately, we kept thinking the camp would be around the next corner, but it never was. Our one hundred metre dash turned into a one thousand metre slog, and we were wet and tired when we crested a final hill and saw the camp across a small stream in a clearing below the pass. Dave, Mark, and André, three fellows who were doing roughly the same journey as ours, were already there and had their tents and a tarp set up. Fortunately for us, the rain decided to let up, and we dubiously inspected the official tent sites. Water had already begun to pool in the gullies and depressions and the mud was annoyingly sticky. We opted for the reasonably level, damp but well-drained patch of grass and plants nearby—a good choice as it turned out. We spent the evening huddled from the rain under the branches of a huge spruce, sharing a portion of the tarp with our three generous fellow travellers.

The next morning, Chad startled his boots with a surprise attack. I again awoke to a terrible pounding sound, and when I peeked out the door of our tent I saw the entire clearing of the campground blanketed in snow and Chad, hunched in the vestibule of his tent, walloping his boots with a large rock. "I'm knocking the frost off," he said, jokingly, "and learnin' 'em some respect."

It was hard to motivate myself to get out of our tent when everything was covered in snow—the trees were covered, the mountains were covered, the ground was covered, and our tent sagged under the ponderous weight of soppy, wet snow. It brought to mind Schäffer's classic observation on weather in 1908. "It is a chronic state of affairs in the Canadian Rockies," she wrote, "that to plan an early trip in them is to court an uncommonly late season, or a heavier snow-fall than has 'ever before been known.' The truth is, the snowfall is always heavy and the season a comparatively short one. . . . Also, no one need ever think he is going to avoid the weather; no mountains were ever made without it, least of all the Rockies."

We packed up quickly and gulped hot coffee, looking around stunned. It wasn't melting. And when we set off it was hard to find the trail. "It's in weather like this that I suddenly wish I was riding a horse," Chad said as we waded a small stream and continued through the snowy field. I had to agree—the idea of the horses' feet getting cold and wet instead of mine was quite appealing. We left the forest behind and approached Maligne Pass in deepening snow and ever colder temperatures. It was winter, and I couldn't blame Don, since he wasn't here. The sky was leaden. Mist crept down, obscuring the peaks. Malevolent-looking clouds clustered to the west, but an optimistic blue gap appeared to the north in the direction we were headed. Perhaps the system had petered out?

The trail was slushy and mucky, and we frequently slipped as we slogged along, grudgingly marveling at the new world of the morning. Chad, however, seemed not at all to mind the slush and inevitable wetness, and indeed seemed to be especially pleased with the day. "The boots," he said, knocking the snow off for our better viewing, "have finally come forward and wish to sit down at the table and sign a treaty, with conditions for surrender."

It was very odd trudging through the barren, windblown, and now totally white pass, hearing the snow crunching under my boots, and at the same time hearing the

Hiking in the slush and snow.

sound of trickling water as rivulets poured in serpentine troughs down from the stony promontories that lined the pass. Two days ago, it had felt like summer, but today it was too cold to linger and enjoy the view, one of Schäffer's favourites. "Reaching the eastern slope," she wrote, "I think I never saw a fairer valley. From our very feet it swept away into an unbroken green carpet as far as the eye could see." As it did for Schäffer in 1908, the world dropped away beneath us. The Maligne Valley stretched away into the distance, an unbroken white carpet.

Descending into the long wilderness valley that leads to Maligne Lake was spiritually uplifting. The snowy trail followed a gurgling stream down into forest, but we enjoyed spectacular views for a long time before reaching the valley bottom. As the day progressed, it warmed up a bit, and the drop in elevation made a significant difference in reducing the snow. By the time we had reached the willow flats a few kilometres from Schäffer Camp, our intended destination, there was no snow, and in fact there may not ever have been any. We enjoyed a quiet night beneath the huge trees around a cheery fire, our boots and socks aligned around it in a steaming circle.

The next day was again cold and overcast and there must have been a "sticking point" in Chad's negotiations with his boots. He devoted an extra twenty minutes to heating them near the small and hastily constructed fire, because the leather had become as stiff as stone after the previous day's soaking. But prevail he did, and with silver tape smothering his feet, he joined me and Steve near the river to start the day's trek. We continued on through the valley, mostly through a thick and loamy forest, surprisingly mossy and damp for Alberta, occasionally emerging into willow flats with prime vistas surrounding us. One of the pleasures of this part of the hike proved to be the quiet remoteness of the valley. Not normally a hiker's favourite because of extensive horse use in the summer, including commercial outfitters, in the fall it seemed to have been left especially for us. We left our boot prints mingled with dozens of elk tracks, and were spooked by frequent encounters with spruce grouse that lazed, camouflaged, on the trail until, at the last possible moment before we trod upon them, they flapped wildly up to nearby branches.

It seemed that we were walking slower than on other days. Each destination seemed further than it should have been; it was only at the end of the day, when we compared our maps and guidebooks, that we realized our planned distance of twenty kilometres was actually twenty-four. It was not a big deal, as twenty-four kilometres can be easily covered in a day, but when we were used to walking at an average speed of no slower than four kilometres an hour, and we found ourselves an hour off, it was somewhat disconcerting, especially for me, the time-keeper of the group. With Mount Unwin behind us, the place where Sid Unwin had first spied the shimmering expanse of Maligne Lake, we emerged from the woods into a clearing before re-entering the forest and beginning the ascent to Evelyn Creek campground, six kilometres distant. We were on our way to the famous Skyline Trail and Schäffer's Shovel Pass.

Moose browsing in the underbrush.

Just before reaching the campsite, Steve spotted a large female moose in a gully adjacent to the trail. She observed us for a moment, perhaps assessing our intentions, before returning to her evening feasting. We took off our packs and sat watching her for about twenty minutes, marvelling at the grace and strength of her movements. For anyone who has never been close to a full grown moose, I can say these animals, although gentle, are huge and unbelievably strong. I felt especially lucky because moose are not very common in the Rocky Mountains. There are only around sixty in all of Jasper National Park, and they are often quite shy of people. After a while, the moose meandered a little further from the trail, and we decided to "keep on keepin' on." In no time, we had arrived. The camp was secluded and sheltered, situated near a clean, clear stream. We were the only people there that night and passed a quiet evening listening to the wind, the creek, and Chad's tales of life in congested Tokyo. I could imagine no more bizarre a juxtaposition.

Evelyn Creek Camp is the first official site along the impressive and often crowded Skyline Trail. Annually around two thousand hikers traverse the forty-four kilometres of the trail, most of it hugging the rocky ridge of the Maligne Range and providing unparalleled vistas, east to the Colin and the Queen Elizabeth Ranges north of Maligne Lake, and west across the Athabasca–Whirlpool Valleys to the range that forms the spine along the Continental Divide. The great, gaping hole in the chain known as Athabasca Pass can be seen southwest from the most prominent height of the ridge. Schäffer, of course, pioneered part of this route when she and her party hauled a survey boat up from near present-day Jasper, over Shovel Pass, and down to Maligne Lake, in 1911. Our plan was to go only as far as Shovel Pass and then follow the steep trail down the western flank of Curator Mountain to Wabasso Lake, where we had left our truck. It was another thirty kilometres or so from Evelyn Creek, up and then steeply down, two more days until we could indulge in the pizza and beer that had come up in conversation with increasing frequency in the last day.

We greeted another cold and dreary day. Hot coffee woke us a little, but the prospect of Kraft Dinner for breakfast, Chad's idea, and the brand name stuff thank goodness, was nevertheless a drag on our enthusiasm. Oddly, it wasn't that bad. Before we finished packing to begin our steep but short hiking day, Chad became extremely dizzy and then ill. He swallowed some Gravol and lay in his tent for a while, the world spinning wildly. He had told us before the trip that he had been having these dizzy episodes for a while, but no one yet knew what caused them. Chad knew they lasted about a day before his balance and strength returned. After some discussion, we decided it would be best if we aborted the remainder of the trip to accompany him back to Maligne Lake. I was sorely disappointed. I had never hiked the Skyline Trail and was eager to see the views from the summit, but it would have to wait for another day. Steve, who had hiked the trail before, assured me that the scenery was spectacular.

Chad proceeded slowly ahead while we packed up our camp and followed hastily behind. Although we considered hiking with him to the parking lot, making sure he found a ride to a hostel, and then returning to complete the trip, we had no idea of the seriousness of his sickness. We felt uncomfortable leaving him on his own, so in the end, we decided to return to Jasper together. It was ironic because, just the day before, we had all been joking about how good it would have been to end the trip early, have hot showers, and eat our long-awaited pizza. But we had geared ourselves up for the final two days, and we were feeling strong. The comforts of civilization, even under

Remembering the glory of Jonas Pass.

these less-than-ideal circumstances, were being achieved sooner than expected. It was somehow sad and anticlimactic, almost as if we didn't deserve comfort yet.

Chad was walking slowly and carefully when we caught up with him, and the three of us eventually made it the six kilometres to the parking lot. As we walked toward the Warden Station, we encountered a young couple from France, who, against all odds, and almost against all common sense I thought at the time, offered to take the three of us, smelly bodies, packs, and all, the long route back to Jasper, and then south to our truck, in their small car. For that, we are eternally grateful. Chad's dizziness improved throughout the day, and later resolved itself without serious consequences. After driving to Whistlers campground and setting up for the evening, the three of us went into town to the aquatic centre where we lounged in a hot tub, and then the steam room, allowing the aches and pains of the previous week to seep out of our bones. We did later have our pizza, in the same restaurant where we had eaten after completing Athabasca Pass earlier in the summer with Mike and Don. That trip seemed a lifetime ago. Out the windows, I could see dark clouds hovering about the ridge of the Skyline, and on a certain level, I was glad to be where I was.

Although we intended to return later in the fall to finish the Skyline, the snows came and we never found the time. The trail remains on my seemingly endless list of wild and wonderful places yet to explore in the mountains. Steve constantly teases me about the unrivalled beauty of the trip. I know he is joking, but I'm sure it is true nonetheless.

Our grand summer of adventure had ended, and, true to our prediction in June, we had experienced our little bit of heaven and our little bit of hell. It was a summer I will always remember. Exploring five forgotten highways, Steve and I had looked into the past and discovered a few of the elusive secrets held by these mountains. Along the way, I had discovered a few secrets about myself. "There are secrets you will never learn," wrote the perceptive Mary Schäffer, "there are some joys you will never feel, there are heart thrills you can never experience, till, with your horse you leave the world, your recognised world, and plunge into the vast unknown." I sincerely hope that the heart of the mountains, far from the congestion and noise along the highways, will always be there when I feel the call, like countless others before me, of the vast unknown.

Epilogue

A NEW JOURNEY BEGINS

everal weeks after our final trek over Maligne Pass, Steve and I embarked on one final excursion before snow plugged the passes for the season. On Thanksgiving weekend, we drove to the Cairns Creek Forest Recreation Site at the end of the Blaeberry logging road, on a pilgrimage to locate the elusive trail over Howse Pass that we had missed in June. Ever a sucker for adventure, Don joined us once again.

"You guys missed it the first time," he said, "so I'd better come along to show you where it is."

Don's presence was especially helpful this time, and not just for his homemade wine and expansive sense of humour. After a summer of over-preparedness, we had at last forgotten something critical. Of the items most vital to any enterprise in the wilds, a backpack within which to store the other items ranks first. Boots, food, and sleeping bags share the second tier. Tent poles also fit into the second tier, and it was tent poles that I could not find. I searched and re-searched the trunk, then burrowed and scrounged in the back seat, as my embarrassment grew. I enlisted Steve's assistance in my quest to no avail. We were both mortified and, finally, I had to admit our predicament to Don, who was lounging by the firepit sipping a cold beer, his spacious tent nicely standing in a small clearing behind him. "How often do I get to rub this in?" Don asked. "It's quite fun to be the hero for a change."

After breakfast the next morning, the three of us hiked back along the David Thompson Heritage Trail through a world entirely changed from what we remembered. The ground was dry. Many of the leaves had fallen, opening up views through the forest, and most significantly, the water levels were so low it made us laugh. I could have forded the Blaeberry River at any point; Cairns Creek was a shadow of its former malevolence, and the swamp where we saw the trail disappear was barely sodden. We found a path leading out of it and up a hill. Although it was in rough condition, grooved by troughs where spring runoff had created channels of a creek, it did indeed lead to the same clearing where we had lost the trail in early July. The swamp that had flooded the clearing was a tiny pond surrounded by brown grasses. After some searching, we found the trail leading to Howse Pass, not entirely obvious even now.

Hoping to prevent others from getting lost as we had, Steve and Don moved several large logs and we made unmistakable arrows on the ground to alert hikers travelling either east or west. I then tied an orange ribbon to a tree on the far side of the seasonal swamp. It seemed the least we could do, remembering our exhausting day of bushwhacking three months before.

That night, as we gathered around the campfire—perched on stumps with our feet stretched to the warmth—our conversation turned to the adventures of the summer. Strongest in my mind that night was an exchange Steve and Chad and I had had at Avalanche Camp near the summit of Maligne Pass. It had been a freezing cold night. We stood shifting around a sputtering, smoky fire with our three campmates, Dave, Mark, and André, while the moon illuminated strange, swirling clouds around the snow-dusted, sombre peaks. We discussed the accomplishments and hardships of the early explorers and travellers—how lucky we were to be able to follow in their footsteps, and in particular, how we have benefited from the labour of early advocates for protected spaces, such as Mary Schäffer. "You have to respect these people," one of them said. "When you think about what they've done . . . you have to respect them and their accomplishments. Really, we should have a moment of reflection, to stop and think of them and thank them for the work they did, so that they're not just forgotten."

Steve, Don, and I had another moment of reflection by our crackling campfire. The season was ending and winter was drawing in. It would be months before we could set off on another backpacking trip. What trails would we explore next year? Even the loquacious Don was quiet, before he poked the fire with a stick, toppling over a burning log and sending sparks into the starry night.

Later that week, I learned that I was pregnant. Steve and I were about to embark on an entirely new kind of adventure.

We are now the parents of two young children. We want to share with our children our love and passion for the Rocky Mountains and for wild places in general. We have already begun. "Those kids," one friend observed, "have had their diapers changed on more mountains than most people hike in their entire lives." We hike at a slower pace these days, and I know that this will continue for some time. For the moment, we are walking along the well-trodden paths of the front-country, rather than the forgotten highways of another era. For our children, discovering these trails is a grand adventure nonetheless, and a stepping stone to future exploration.

Our greatest hope is that as a society we will continue to have the courage to shield the heart of the mountains, this untamed island in an overly developed world, to preserve the region not as a museum, but as a place future generations can come, to explore on foot or on horseback, as people have done for thousands of years.

Further Reading

Fraser, Esther. *The Canadian Rockies: Early Travels and Explorations*. Calgary: Fifth House, 2002. Reprint of a 1969 original.

Gadd, Ben. *Handbook of the Canadian Rockies*. Jasper: Corax Press, 1995.

Hart, E.J. *The Place of Bows: Exploring the Heritage of the Banff-Bow Valley*. Banff: EJH Literary Enterprises, Ltd. 1999.

Jenish, D'Arcy. *Epic Wanderer: David Thompson and the Mapping of the Canadian West*. Toronto: Doubleday Canada, 2003.

Palliser, John and James Hector. *The Journals, Detailed Reports, and Observations Relative to the Exploration by Captain John Palliser During the Years 1857, 1858, 1859, and 1860*. London: Eyre & Spottiswoode, 1863.

Patton, Brian. *Tales from the Canadian Rockies*. Edmonton: Hurtig Publishers, 1984.

Sandford Beck, Janice. *No Ordinary Woman: The Story of Mary Schäffer Warren*. Calgary: Rocky Mountain Books, 2001.

Schäffer, Mary T.S. *Old Indian Trails of the Canadian Rockies*. New York: G.P. Putnam's Sons, 1911.

Simpson, Sir George. *Narrative of a Journey Round the World during the years 1841 and 1842*. London: Henry Colburn, 1874.

Simpson, George, Frederick Merk, Ed. *Fur Trade and Empire—George Simpson's Journal*. Cambridge: Harvard University Press, 1931.

Spry, Irene M. *The Palliser Expedition: The Dramatic Story of Western Canadian Exploration, 1857-1860*. Toronto: MacMillan, 1963. Republished by Fifth House Publishers, 1995.

Thompson, David, J.B. Tyrell, Ed. *David Thompson's Narrative of His Explorations in Western America, 1784-1812*. Toronto: The Champlain Society, 1916.

Thompson, David, Barbara Belyea, Ed. *David Thompson's Columbia Journals*. Montreal: McGill-Queen's University Press, 1994.

Binnema, Theodore. "How Does a Map Mean?: Old Swan's Map of 1801 and the Blackfoot World," in *From Rupert's Land to Canada*. Edmonton: University of Alberta Press, 2001.

Van Tighem, Kevin. *Bears*. Canmore: Altitude Publishing, 1999.

—To see the *Forgotten Highways* photos in colour, please visit www.stephenrbown.net

Acknowledgements

We would like to thank the following businesses that donated supplies to assist us with our research and travel: Banff Book & Art Den, for books on Rocky Mountain history and contemporary hiking guides; Eureka, for a magnificent tent that kept us dry through many a storm and backpacks that easily withstood an intense summer of abuse; Soft Path Cuisine, for the delicious dehydrated meals that fueled us along each journey (www.softpathcuisine.com); and GemTrek Maps, for a complete collection of their excellent maps of the Rocky Mountains. We would also like to thank Arcteryx and Sierra Designs.

On the writing side of things, we would like to acknowledge the support we received from the Alberta Foundation for the Arts. We would also like to thank our agents Frances and Bill Hanna of Acacia House Publishing for keeping faith with this project in the long search for a publisher, and Ruth Linka of Brindle & Glass for understanding the book and agreeing to publish it—and then selecting Linda Goyette as editor. Thank you, Linda, for intuitively understanding our manuscript and urging us to personalize it with more dialogue and humour. A huge thanks to Steve's brother David Bown and his business High Country Web Design (www.high-country.ca), who, in addition to designing and maintaining the website (www.stephenrbown.net), slaved over the beautiful maps that illustrate each of our journeys. And thanks also to Doug Whiteway of *The Beaver* for commissioning a couple of articles based on our research.

Last, but not least, thanks to our intrepid fellow adventurers, in particular Don Baird, for putting up with a summer of often awful weather, and keeping us laughing even years later.

Nicky Brink is a research lawyer, originally from Toronto, she lived in Kingston, St. John's, Vancouver, and Ottawa before settling in the Canadian Rockies. An avid backpacker and traveller, she has hiked on trails from Newfoundland to British Columbia and the Yukon. She thought history was boring, until she met Stephen on a hike to the historic Cabot Tower atop Signal Hill in St. John's. Since then she has edited dozens of Stephen's history-related articles and books and came up with the idea for *Forgotten Highways*. She and Stephen live in Canmore with their two young children.

Stephen R. Bown has been writing about adventurers, travellers, and explorers for years in magazines and is a frequent contributor to *The Beaver* (Canada's History Magazine). His book *Scurvy: How a Surgeon, a Mariner and a Gentleman Solved the Greatest Medical Mystery of the Age of Sail* was an international critical success and was selected as one of the *Globe and Mail's* Top 100 Books of 2004. His most recent book *A Most Damnable Invention: Dynamite, Nitrates and the Making of the Modern World* was short-listed for the Wilfrid Eggleston Award for Non-Fiction and the Canadian Science Writers Association Science in Society Book Award. He is currently writing a biography: *Agent of Empire: Discovery, Madness and Scandal — the Tragic Fate of Captain George Vancouver and the Struggle for Pacific America*. His website is: www.stephenrbown.net.